Mojave National Preserve

Other books from Olympus Press include

Mojave

NATIONAL PRESERVE
A Visitor's Guide

Cheri Rae & John McKinney

Olympus Press
SANTA BARBARA

Portions of this book were previously published as *East Mojave Desert: A Visitor's Guide* published by Olympus Press in 1989, *Walking the East Mojave Desert* published by HarperCollins in 1994, and in numerous articles in the *Los Angeles Times*.

Book Design & Typography by Jim Cook

Cover Art: Marianne D. Wallace

Cartography: Susan Kuromiya

ACKNOWLEDGMENTS

For their considerable efforts in field- and fact-checking this guide, our thanks to the staff of Mojave National Preserve, including Superintendent Mary Martin, Chief Ranger Sean McGuinness, James Woolsey, Ruby Newton, Welford Garner, Dennis Schramm, and Jean de los Reyes.

For their collective enthusiasm for interpretive efforts on behalf of Mojave National Preserve, as well as their support for this guide, we thank members of the Death Valley Natural History Association and salute the association's Board members and Executive Director Janice Newton. For their conservation efforts past and present, we'd like to thank the chairs of the California Desert Protection League: Judy Anderson, Elden Hughes, and Jim Dodson. For their help with an earlier edition of this guide, and for hiking with us in searing heat and unexpected snowstorms, thanks to Jim Foote, Harold Johnson and John Bailey of the U.S. Bureau of Land Management. For Old West hospitality, a tip of the that to Jerry Freeman and Roxanne Lang.

PHOTO CREDITS

Automobile Club of Southern California 85, 94, 95; California Department of Parks & Recreation 175, 176; California State Library 41, 62; Desert Studies Center 156; Lake Dolores Waterpark 108; Mojave River Valley Museum: J. Amari Collection 100; Billingham Collection 96; Bruce Collection 58, 59; Cochran Collection 65; Burnau Pendergast Collection 72; Pinnell Collection 178; Mary Beal Collection 183; Brenck Collection 212, 213; MacFarlane Collection 122, 260; MacFarlane/Prather Collection 232 (top); Mojave River Valley Museum Collection 147, 160; National Park Service 9, 52, 134, 162 (bottom), 164; San Bernardino County Library, Needles 56, 119; Steele Photographic Service 66, 67, 102, 162 (top), 186, 193, 200, 214; U.S. Bureau of Land Management 33, 36, 37, 44 (top), 48, 50, 54, 55, 105, 118, 130, 139, 161, 189, 206 (bottom). All other photos by John McKinney.

MOJAVE NATIONAL PRESERVE: A VISITORS GUIDE

Foreword

While working at National Park Service headquarters in Washington D.C., my thoughts often drifted to the wide open spaces and grand landscapes of the American West. I grew up in the West, and the mountains, forests and deserts have long occupied a special place in my heart. When the opportunity arose for me to become superintendent of the new Mojave National Preserve, I leaped at the chance to get back into the field.

Oh, what a "field" to supervise! For starters, 1.6-million acre Mojave National Preserve is the third largest national park land in the continental U.S. (only Yellowstone National Park and nearby Death Valley National Park are larger).

Within the boundaries of this vast new national parkland is a diversity of desert landforms—from the mirage-like Soda Lake to the shifting Kelso Dunes, and from Table Mountain to Hole-in-the-Wall. The world's largest Joshua tree forest, eerie extinct volcanoes, and a dozen dramatic mountain ranges add to Mojave's considerable allure. Bighorn sheep gambol about the craggy peaks and the venerable desert tortoise moves slowly across the valley floors.

Things are a bit different out here. Because Mojave National Preserve is so new, don't expect the kind of visitor services common to a national park that's been in existence for 75 years: a big visitor center, huge campgrounds, lots and lots of signs. The National Park Service has improved Mojave's modest-sized campgrounds, posted some key signs, and is constructing a visitor center at the old Kelso Depot; however, no large-scale park development projects are in the works, and our intention is to keep the sense of adventure that makes a visit to the preserve such a special experience.

With a thousand miles of desert roads and hundreds of natural attractions beckoning, you might not know where to begin your exploration, and that's how *Mojave National Preserve: A Visitor's Guide* will help you out. Authors Cheri Rae and John McKinney have been writing about the wonders of this desert, and championing its preservation, for more than a decade. Preserve staff was pleased to lend its expertise in support of this book, an excellent introduction to a wondrous land.

As you discover the preserve's spectacular wildflower displays, follow the historic trails of Native Americans and the pioneers, and gaze up at night skies amass with twinkling stars, I hope you'll come to love and appreciate Mojave, as well as to understand why its preservation was so critical.

MARY G. MARTIN, *Superintendent*
Mojave National Preserve

Introduction

Mojave National Preserve is a vast, mountainous land that represents a meeting of three great deserts—the Great Basin, Sonoran and Mojave. This meeting and mixing of desert ecosystems produces a wide variety of flora in combinations that exist nowhere else in the world.

Mojave is home to creatures both slow and swift—the desert tortoise and desert bighorn sheep—and to the largest and densest population of Joshua trees. Every feature visitors associate with the desert (sand dunes, grand mesas, dry lake beds, mountain ranges and more) is present in Mojave National Preserve, along with some features visitors usually don't associate with a desert: limestone caves, lava flows and cinder cones.

Mojave is a preserve of unusual diversity, a land that's easy to like, difficult to know. While the vastness of this land can intimidate, by exploring Mojave National Preserve a little at a time, you'll soon come to know and love this special place. It's a half-day's drive from the metropolis, a world apart.

The intent of this guide is to help you explore this vast unknown land. In the past, information about this desert has been as scarce as water in these parts. While the area, prior to the creation of Mojave National Preserve in 1994, often made the news over such controversies as mining activity, off-highway vehicle use, and whether the desert should be "upgraded" to national park status, these headlines offered few clues to its beauty and recreational possibilities.

In addition to providing an introduction to the scenery, an attempt has been made to mine Mojave's rich legends and lore. This land was once populated far more extensively than it is now (quite the reverse of most of the rest of California!) and the colorful characters who lived and worked here are a book in themselves.

In 1980, the eastern Mojave gained national prominence when Congress set aside 1.5 million acres in the California desert and designated it the East Mojave National Scenic Area. It was the first of the nation's Scenic Areas (among other areas later set aside were Mono Lake, the Santa Rosa Mountains and the Columbia River Gorge). The scenic area was assigned to the U.S. Bureau of Land Management, an agency under the Department of the Interior.

While "National Scenic Area" status put the East Mojave on the map as something special, the designation lacked the allure to most Americans of those two magic words: "National Park." Visitation remained light (though annually increasing) during the 1980s and early 1990s.

Two groups that did not ignore—and, in fact, obsessed about—Mojave were planners and politicians. Planners, both governmental and environmental advocates, compiled massive documents about what all of us— miners, motorists, mountain climbers and more—would/could/should do in the desert. Planners, in the peculiar jargon of their trade, spoke of UPAS (Unusual Plant Assemblages), WSAs (Wilderness Study Areas) and FLPMA (Federal Land Policy and Management Act), as in "How will we manage the UPAS in the WSAs under FLMPA?"

Politicians (particularly California's U.S. senators) continually beat the drum for more (or less) federal protection for the desert. Lobbyists for ranching and mining interests, the Sierra Club and the National Rifle Association, and many more special-interest groups, tried to convince legislators of their particular views toward the eastern Mojave.

Ultimately after nearly two decades of politicking, Congress passed legislation establishing Mojave National Preserve and transferred responsibility for its administration to the National Park Service. The eleventh-hour compromise to create a preserve instead of a park reflected the extremely complex and often bitter battle for passage of the California Desert Protection Act. Differences between a national park and national preserve are few, and will be explored later this guide.

Now that this land is under the stewardship of the National Park Service, how many of us actually visit Mojave National Preserve? A truly accurate count is all but impossible because unlike some popular western national parks where visitors pass through toll gates, and bureaucrats measure use in millions of "visitor days," no one in this vast desert collects admission fees. Additionally, Mojave has many entrances—making a visitor count difficult.

According to a recent National Park Service survey, some 64 percent of Mojave visitors are Californians and 11 percent are Nevadans. About 18 percent of Mojave visitors hail from all the rest of the states combined, and seven percent of visitors come from foreign countries. Visitors from faraway states, as well as from distant countries, are increasing rapidly as word of Mojave's attractions spreads across the nation and around the world.

During the late 1990s, visitation was about evenly split between first-timers and repeat visitors. As expected, Southern Californians visit in great numbers; more surprisingly, considering the greater distance, San Francisco Bay area residents are a not-so-distant second in visitor numbers.

Some 61 percent of Mojave visitors report that sightseeing by car is their principal preserve activity, while half say they come to Mojave for nature study and hiking. About 32 percent of visitors say they want to see historic sites, and 22 percent come to camp. More than half of preserve visitors make the pilgrimage to Kelso

Depot and Kelso Dunes while only four percent tour Soda Springs/Zzyzx.

Annual visitation is extremely difficult to calculate not only because of the many entryways to the preserve, but also due to the difficulty in distinguishing sightseeing visitors from "drive-throughs." (Death Valley National Park and Joshua Tree National Park visitor counters have similar difficulty.) In high season (March), vehicle entries exceed those made in July (definitely not a time to visit!) by only 20 percent. However, many more visitors are likely to get out of their cars and linger during the height of spring than in the dead of summer.

Massive population growth has occurred in the nation's desert lands since the development and widespread use of air-conditioning. For several decades, Los Angeles has spilled from its core coastal basin into the desert to the north—Palmdale, Lancaster, Victorville and throughout the Antelope Valley—and to the east—Banning, Palm Springs, Indio, and throughout the Coachella Valley. San Diego suburbs, too, have spread east from the coast deep into the desert.

The desert-directed expansion of California's two largest cities has been well charted and is often not as surprising to observers as the phenomenal growth of Las Vegas, currently the fastest-growing urban area in the nation. Las Vegas and vicinity, growing by more than 5,000 new arrivals per month, now has a population of more than 1.2 million.

Given the astronomical population growth that's occurred, and that forecast to take place in the 21st century, Mojave National Preserve will be all the more valuable an environment and recreation area in the years to come.

ACCESS

Mojave National Preserve is bounded north and south by two major Interstates, I-15 and I-40, and on the east by U.S. Highway 95. (Just south of I-40 is one of the longest remaining stretches of old Route 66.) The area bounded by these three highways has been dubbed "The Lonesome Triangle."

Motorists who speed along these superhighways in air-conditioned comfort rarely think of the sturdy pioneers who made their way across this barren territory a century ago. These pioneers knew there were no supply outlets where they could expect to reprovision along the way, so they carried sufficient food and water.

Desert towns have since mushroomed, and services have been established in many places throughout the Mojave; still, some modern-day travelers express reluctance to venture into the desert. While it's true that services are widely spaced in the desert, undue concern about becoming stranded far from civilization is largely unwarranted.

Access roads to Mojave National Preserve pass through many small towns, where essentials—food, gas, water, telephones—are

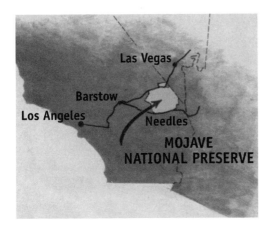

available. Good planning and advance preparation, and perhaps some on-the-spot resourcefulness will enrich your Mojave adventure.

Desert drivers often complain that the long, straight and virtually unchanging highway is monotonous and boring to drive. Your travel through the desert is more pleasant, however, when you take a little time to explore the sights located right off the highway. Several chapters in this guide help you do just that. On the way to Mojave National Preserve, visit a beautiful canyon, an archeological excavation site, a fossil-laden ancient lake bed—even old-time diners and abandoned gas stations along historic old Route 66.

Remember, it's all a matter of perspective: one person's interminable stretch of highway is another's road to adventure. The journey can be as important—and as enjoyable—as the destination.

About this Book

"**B**ig sand!" shouts Daniel, our two-year-old son, as he slips and slides along the steep southeast face of the Kelso Dunes.

"Like Pismo Dunes," chimes in Sophia, our seven-year-old daughter, as she takes her brother's hand and hauls him toward the top. "Except these dunes touch the sky."

As we near the crest of the dunes, our footsteps cause mini-avalanches and the dunes sha-boom sha-boom for us. Geologists speculate that the extreme dryness of this desert, combined with the wind-polished, well-rounded grains of sands, has something to do with their musical ability. Sometimes the low rumbling sound reminds us of a Tibetan gong, but on this particular day the sound is like a 1950s *doo-wop* group.

We have a 45-square-mile formation of magnificently sculpted sand, the most extensive dune field in the West, all to ourselves. We're surprised at such solitude; after all, it's been more than five years since Mojave National Preserve was formed.

Of course, we can't contemplate the quiet of the dunes as easily as we used to—not over the exuberant shouts and joyful noise of our children. Still, their commotion causes barely a ripple in this usually silent land.

Our family has an intense history with this part of the California desert. The quietude of the dunes this time was in complete contrast to our first visit here on Thanksgiving weekend, 1987, when we (nature writer John McKinney and magazine editor Cheri Rae) toured the East Mojave on a press trip with then-Senator Alan Cranston, who had just introduced his California Desert Protection Bill in Congress.

One of the bill's provisions proposed transfer of the East Mojave National Scenic Area, as it was then called, from the U.S. Bureau of Land Management to the National Park Service. The measure was controversial, to say the least. Outspoken park supporters and outspoken park opposers badgered Senator Cranston and anyone else who would listen.

The senator had long championed the eastern Mojave and his "fam" (familiarization) trips had become legend among conservationists and infamous among those who wanted less, not more, protection for the desert. We were heartened to witness our aging senator fighting a last environmental battle. It takes a special person to recognize the value of a desert—much less one largely unknown to the public—and then to insist on making it a national park.

By the time we started hiking up Kelso Dunes, we had thrust upon us a day pack full of position papers, from the Sierra Club to the mining industry, from the Wilderness Society to off-road vehicle boosters.

And so we fell in step-in more ways than one. Ascending the dunes to escape the political din, the newly introduced couple was filled with inspiration. "All that arguing about a land nobody's seen," Cheri commented. "I'll bet if more people experienced the magic of this place, the eastern Mojave would become a national park."

"That's for sure," John agreed. "All we ever hear about on the news is that ridiculous Barstow to Las Vegas motorcycle race through Mojave; nothing about this land's beauty or the sights to see."

That day we began a relationship with the eastern Mojave that continues to this day. We explored this desert from Aiken Wash to Zzyx, and we fell in love.

It seems we spent half our courtship working to produce a map that illustrated this land, and publishing an earlier version of the guidebook you're holding in your hands. We wanted others to experience this exquisite desert land that's attracted curious travelers, fortune seekers and romantic adventurers. And we wanted others to join us in working to protect and preserve Mojave.

We both admit to a long-held appreciation for California's dry lands. Native Californians, we grew up cherishing our Golden State—its colorful history and diverse beauty. We both spent a great deal of time exploring the deserts of our home state.

John spent his boyhood as a Scout and counts his Mojave camping and hiking experiences as some of his most enjoyable. Cheri fondly remembers her extended family's "jackrabbit homesteads," where her immigrant grandparents and all their brothers and sisters bought plots of land in Yucca Valley, and recreated a California desert version of their village in Sicily.

We discovered that Kelso Dunes is a place where yellow desert primrose, pink sand verbena and even romance blossoms. Our daughter discovered desert pleasures when she was still a babe in arms, and now for the first time we've brought our young son along to experience Mojave National Preserve. As we watch Daniel and Sophia slide down the dunes, the joy for us is repeated as our children absorb the spirit of this place.

Back in 1987 when we talked of establishing Mojave as a national park for future generations the notion was a bit abstract; we didn't quite imagine little nature lovers of our own would be a part of that future.

Years later, we're proud to share what we know about this larger-than-life landscape with our children and yours, with this generation and the ones to follow. We hope that in some small way our efforts have contributed to the preservation, and continued good stewardship of what our young son calls "the Big Sand."

Part I

Getting to Know the Land

1

The Land

I f this land could speak, what stories it would tell! Tales of Indians and Spanish explorers, trappers and trailblazers, pioneers and gold miners, cattle ranchers and restless spirits. It would speak of the past, when rugged individualists and determined families lived harmoniously with this place; working hard with their hands, traversing it quietly, carefully, with a little fear and a lot of respect, and leaving behind little more than tracks in the sand. It would tell of booms and busts, lone prospectors and great armies, those who scratched at the land and scarred it, those who lived with the land and loved it.

If this land could speak, it would remind us, we last-minute arrivals on the scene, that it has witnessed profound changes in form and substance, change by firestorm and flood and the passage of millions of years. It would speak of the great oceans and tropical forests that once covered it and speak of the cactus and creosote, jimson and juniper and the thousand and one living things that bloom and blossom and cover it today. It would speak of the great numbers of animals that have inhabited this place— some now extinct, others whose very existence is endangered.

Yet this land that cannot speak calls to us. Some of us have been drawn to its silent places, some of us have let the desert fill our hearts. It's a call of the wild that can't be heard, only felt and experienced.

So it's we humans who speak, sometimes eloquently, sometimes with great disregard for the beauty of the English language, for this land. Today, the silent places are often the subject of noisy debate among miners, ranchers, environmentalists, fundamentalists, land planners, politicians, actors and actresses, off-road vehicle riders, rockhounds, birdwatchers, hikers, mountain bikers, motorcyclists, herpetologists, photographers, astronomers . . . in short, just about everyone who has ever set foot in the desert has an opinion about this land, how it should be managed and who should manage it.

"If you would experience a landscape, you must go alone into it and sit down somewhere quietly and wait for it to come in its own good time to you," writes Paul Gruchow in *The Necessity of Empty Places*. We propose that you visit some of the silent places of Mojave National Preserve— and take your own sweet time of it.

When the land speaks to you and you are moved—and you will be moved because no one who visits the wonders of this desert land is left unmoved—you, too, will want to speak for the land. And when you speak we hope it is with a clear voice, a strong voice, a voice that speaks from the heart of the beauty you have seen and of the necessity for preserving this beauty in a world that has already lost far too many wild, beautiful silent places.

MOJAVE: WORLD HISTORY IN THE ROCKS

The Mojave is far from the world's largest or most severe desert, but it's surely one of the most geologically fascinating. Geologists like this desert because the land is naked, exposed. Recorded in the ancient rocks and vast sands is the history of the world.

For geologists, Mojave National Preserve is a showcase of ancient and modern formations, as well as both slow and sudden processes. *Mojave National Preserve: 2.7 Billion Years In The Making* would be the title of a movie made about how Mojave's landscapes came to be. Rocks tell the stories of a land that's more than half the age of Planet Earth.

The 54,000-square-mile Mojave is the

smallest of the four North American deserts. It's situated south of the Great Basin, north of the Sonoran, and northwest of the Chihuahuan. Its elevation ranges primarily from 2,000 to 4,000 feet, although it includes both the lowest point in the United States, at Badwater in Death Valley (282 feet below sea level) and many mountain peaks above 7,000 feet. Southern Californians often call it "the high desert" because of its elevation.

The topography of the Mojave is termed "basin and range." It is characterized by south-trending mountain ranges rising abruptly from the desert floor, separated by irregularly spaced basins. (Basins, unlike valleys, are not drained by rivers.) The mountains have been formed by the movement of the land along earthquake faults that run through here.

While deserts can be cool, warm, hot or very hot, the common factor among all of them is dryness. Technically, a desert is a land that receives less than ten inches of precipitation annually; its evaporation rate usually exceeds the amount of precipitation. The Mojave averages less than six inches of precipitation, most of which occurs during the winter months, often in the form of snowfall.

Temperature extremes are characteristic of deserts—not only from summer to winter, but from day to night. During the summer, it's not uncommon for the temperature to fluctuate fifty degrees in twenty-four hours. During the day, the surface of the soil absorbs most of the incoming solar radiation because there is so little humidity and so little vegetation to deflect it. At night, heat rapidly dissipates as it's re-radiated back to the sky.

The mountain ranges to the west and south of the Mojave are responsible for the dryness of the desert. As warm, moist ocean air cools, it rises up the slopes of the Tehachapi, Sierra Nevada, San Gabriel, San Bernardino and San Jacinto ranges, and dumps rain and snow on the western slopes. As the air flows down the east side, it becomes warmer and drier. Deserts situated on the east side of coastal mountains are termed "rainshadow deserts."

The mountains also cause the ever-present afternoon winds in the Mojave. Air movement occurs to equalize temperature difference between the mountains and the comparatively warmer desert floor. These winds tend to dissipate by nightfall, but not before they dry the air and erode the surfaces of the land, distributing natural materials and debris in their wake.

THE MOJAVE DESERT—EAST AND WEST

The West Mojave is that part of the desert bounded on the east by the Mojave River. It sweeps north and west from Barstow toward Death Valley and the southern Sierra Nevada.

The West Mojave takes in the burgeoning Antelope Valley, including Lancaster and

Victorville. The East is the larger part of the Mojave and extends east to the Nevada border and to the Colorado River.

Topographically, the East and West Mojave are quite different. The West presents great sandscapes, with many flat areas and some isolated ridges and buttes. The East Mojave, too, has its flatlands—primarily in the form of big basins and wide valleys between mountain ranges, but it is the mountain ranges themselves that differentiate the East Mojave from other desert lands.

The East Mojave represents a time scale almost beyond human comprehension. From the granite formations of Mesozoic Age—more than 150 million years old—to young 10 million year old Cenozoic rocks, the igneous, metamorphic and sedimentary rocks reveal a long and complex past.

During more recent geological time, some 20,000 years ago, this land was covered with abundant waters, rivers and lakes. Marshlands, grassy valleys and stands of pines, junipers and oaks sheltered a wide array of mammals and birds. Fossil remains of extinct sloth, camels, bison and enormous prehistoric horses are evidence of a very different land than we see here today.

But approximately 11,000 years ago, the weather became drier and warmer; as the lakes dried up, the forests and grasslands shriveled away and died. With their food supply depleted, many of the animals also perished. Native people seeking available food and water migrated throughout the area. In true Darwinian fashion, all life in the rapidly growing desert became a matter of survival of the fittest.

As life forms have changed over the ages so, too, has the land. Hot, dry winds have eroded mountains into grains of sand, then built them up again as sand dunes. Runoff from irregular, but violent, thunderstorms has carved canyons and washes; debris carried down from the mountains by the turgid waters has built up fanlike formations. Volcanic activity has created cinder cones, spectacular rock formations and lava flows, and geologic movement along faults has crumpled, folded and tipped this stratified land. These natural forces have created dramatic geographic features, unique in all the world.

Cholla gardens and tabletop mountains, combined with clear skies and fluffy clouds – just another day in Mojave National Preserve.

A DESERT OF MOUNTAINS

It's often said that the eastern Mojave, and Mojave National Preserve in particular, is a desert of mountains. These mountains are situated along north-south trending faults. A glance at a map indicates chains of mountain ranges throughout the area. Especially prominent is the southwest-northeast trending chain formed by the Granite, Providence, Mid Hill and New York ranges.

Ranging from southeast to northwest are the Sacramento, Bristol and Old Dad Mountain ranges; ranging from north to south are the Piutes and Ivanpahs.

The rugged ranges of Mojave National Preserve have been highly eroded; characteristic of this action is the buildup of loose sedimentary materials at the base of the mountains.

These apron-shaped formations are

called alluvial fans. When alluvial fans grow so large that they begin to converge and fill in the distance between them, they are called bajadas.

VOLCANIC FORMATIONS

Located in the northwest section of the preserve is the 25,600-acre area known as the "Cinder Cones National Natural Landmark." The 32 conical-shaped cinder cone formations that comprise this landmark are actually extinct volcanoes. Some were formed fairly recently—within the last 1,000 years—while others date back nearly ten million years. Black basalt, material thrown out by the erupting cones, has built up a thick layer on an underlying granite base.

The lunar-like landscape of the cinder cone area – a National Natural Landmark

East of the cinder cones is the 75-square-mile formation known as Cima Dome. While not technically a volcanic formation, Cima Dome is the result of a huge uplift of molten rock. It's been eroded over the years, and today appears as an almost-perfectly symmetrical granite formation that rises gently above the surrounding area.

Castle Peaks—jagged, red-colored, spire-like formations that rise steeply from the surrounding New York Mountains—are volcanic in nature. The mysterious towers near Hole-in-the-Wall campground, along with the Swiss-cheese-shaped rocks in nearby Banshee Canyon, are other examples of vulcanism.

BASIN, RANGE AND MORE

Dry lake beds, or playas, are characteristic of basin and range lands. Remnants of lakes that evaporated long ago, these flat areas are highly alkaline, and support few forms of life. Soda Dry Lake, located on the western boundary of the Mojave National Preserve, is a very large playa that can become wet when rainfall is significant.

Dry washes, also called arroyos, are cut by water scouring the desert floor. They look like dry streambeds, but they can rapidly become raging waterways—flash floods—during thunderstorms or significant rainfalls. Although it may seem that the wind is the dominant cause of erosion in the desert, the presence of water—occasional though it may be—actually sculpts and carves the land to a more significant

degree. Flash floods can swiftly carry rocks, boulders, branches, sand and silt, depositing the materials far from where they were originally picked up by the rushing waters.

Desert varnish, a distinctive, shiny, dark-brown coating that appears on rocks, occurs when manganese and iron are present; it may also be related to the presence of acids that occur during the decomposition of lichen.

Desert pavement, also called desert mosaic, is the cemented-together surface of closely fitted rocks, pebbles and gravel and other materials. This hard, flat surface is created by a combination of wind and rain moving the small rocks, and flushing away the fine soil.

Tabletop mesas occur throughout Mojave, the most distinctive of which is known as Table Mountain, a 6,176-foot mesa.

Of all the distinctive natural features in the desert, perhaps none is more deeply moving than the special quality of the light, the vastness of the sky. Poets and writers have long recorded the magnificence of the opalescent light, the spectacular sunrises and sunsets. For city dwellers all too accustomed to viewing murky night skies, gazing at the Milky Way on display is a revelation and a truly awesome experience. This is a place where shooting stars and constellations appear with startling clarity. Study your sky charts and bring your telescopes; the night sky is as dramatic here as it gets.

2

Plants & Animals

In his classic turn-of-the-century book, *The Desert,* John C. Van Dyke wrote, "Nature does not bend the elements to favor the plants and animals; she makes the plants and the animals do the bending." Life in the desert requires adaptation, not only for visitors, but for vegetation and wildlife as well.

Successful desert plants and animals have adjusted to conditions that seem designed to forbid any form of life. Unique, specifically adapted plants and animals have developed in spite of temperature extremes, intense sunlight, fierce and frequent winds, and long periods of drought.

Most people think of deserts as barren wastelands, devoid of life except for a cactus or two. But most desert areas support diverse populations of plants and animals. The varied landforms and range of altitudes in Mojave, as well as the localized presence of water, create a number of specific ecological communities.

Mojave National Preserve is an exciting place for botanists and biologists because the area is so vast and uncharted and because of the possibility of discovering new life forms. Two University of California herpetologists recently discovered a new species of western toad, and species of Jerusalem cricket have turned up in the sand dunes.

Enthusiasm in the scientific community is tempered with worry about the effects of human intrusion into the desert world. Gone from the Mojave, from the earth, are the Tecopa pupfish, the Mojave tarplant and more. Researchers say we don't know enough about the desert to know what is being lost.

"We don't know that much about the desert, and we ought to preserve it so future generations have some options," declares Gerald Scherba, a biologist formerly with the Desert Sudies Center in Zzyzx. "Unless you absolutely need a resource, the prudent thing is to leave it alone."

JOSHUA TREE–HIGH DESERT WOODLAND

Probably the most distinctive of the Mojave Desert communities, the Joshua tree woodland is found at altitudes from 2,500 to 4,500 feet, on well-drained desert slopes. In Mojave, the Joshua tree woodland can be found at Cima Dome, Ivanpah Valley and Lanfair Valley.

The Joshua tree, with its upturned branches is easily recognized but not always admired. Explorer John C. Frémont called it "the most repulsive tree in the vegetable kingdom." Writer Charles Francis Saunders noted, "The trees themselves were as grotesque as the creations of a bad dream; the shaggy trunks and limbs were twisted and seemed writhing as though in pain, and dagger-pointed leaves were clenched in bristling fists of inhospitality." And Joseph Smeaton Chase, who hardly ever met a tree he didn't like, wrote, "It is a weird, menacing object, more like some conception of Poe's or Doré's than any work of wholesome Mother Nature. One can scarcely find a term of ugliness that is not apt for this plant. A misshapen pirate with belts, boots, hands, and teeth stuck full of daggers is as near as I can come to a human analogy. The wood is a harsh, rasping fibre; knife-blades, long, hard and keen, fill the place of leaves; the flower is greenish white and ill-smelling; and the fruit a cluster of nubbly pods, bitter and useless. A landscape filled with Joshua trees has a nightmare effect even in broad daylight; at the witching hour it can be almost infernal."

Despite the unflattering descriptions, the Joshua tree and surrounding community do have their attractions. The dramatic colors of the sky at sunset provide a breathtaking backdrop for the world's largest Joshua tree forest which grows on Cima Dome.

While the Joshuas at Cima are the most numerous, the individual trees are not among the tallest of trees. Two subspecies of Joshua trees thrive in the Mojave Desert, and the one in the preserve—*yucca brevifolia Jaegeriana*—is the shorter of the two. The other type, taller and with longer leaves, is found in Joshua Tree National Park.

The Joshua tree provides shelter for a number of small desert animals, particularly rodents, such as the kangaroo rat, desert wood rat, and ground squirrel. Birds, including the pinyon jay, loggerhead shrike and Scott's oriole, make their nests in the gnarled branches. Reptiles inhabiting the community include the chuckwalla, desert night lizard and desert tortoise. The yucca moth enjoys a symbiotic relationship with the Joshua tree. The moth fertilizes the trees' flowers by transporting pollen from stamen to pistil; some of the germinated seeds then serve as food for the moth larvae.

Other members of the Joshua tree woodland include: Barrel cactus, chollas, hedgehog cactus, and beavertail cactus, as well as the Mojave yucca, California juniper, Utah juniper, paperbag bush, spiny tetradymia, desert bunch grass, galleta bladder sage, creosote bush and buckwheat.

Hardly a barren land, Mojave supports an abundance of diverse flora.

CREOSOTE BUSH–LOW DESERT SCRUB

This drought-tolerant community is the most common in Mojave, found primarily in the low, dry valleys at less than 2,000 or 3,000 feet in elevation. A particularly good example thrives in Wild Horse Canyon, near Hole-in-the-Wall. Most of the creosote bush community consists of widely spaced shrubs which grow three to six feet tall.

The creosote bush, which is the most recognizable plant in this community, is a hardy plant that withstands prolonged periods of drought. The creosote bush is often called "greasewood" for the resinous substance that coats its leaves. The plant has a pungent, distinctive odor; the Spanish word for it, *Hediondilla,* means "little stinker." Although it is a scrubby bush, the creosote has an extensive root system which searches out any available moisture. The creosote

Teddy bear cholla

bushes growing in Soggy Dry Lake (south-west of Mojave National Preserve), are said to be the world's oldest living things. Called King Clone, they are estimated to be more than 10,000 years old.

Also characteristic of this community is the so-called "Devil's Garden," a grouping of several types of cactus interspersed with boulders and other rock formations.

Other members of the community include brittlebush, desert mallow, ocotillo, burrobush, indigo bush, dye bush, desert lily, Bigelow's cholla, silver cholla, teddy bear and buckhorn cholla, and pincushion.

As a result of his frequent encounters with cholla, author Joseph Smeaton Chase disdained it and wrote in his classic *California Desert Trails:* "It is an ugly object three of four feet high, with stubby arms standing out like amputated stumps. . . . The Indians say that they jump at you: this sounds like an exaggeration, but upon my word I don't know. Often when I have felt sure that I passed clear of a certain cholla I found he had me after all." Careless or unsuspecting hikers, beware.

Many of the animals that inhabit this community are small, nocturnal rodents and are rarely seen by desert visitors. Instead, the presence of the animals—ground squirrel, jackrabbit, kangaroo rat, and pocket mouse—is indicated by their tracks.

More easily observed species include several birds: the roadrunner, Costa's hum-

Desert author Joseph Smeaton Chase (*California Desert Trails,* 1919) usually had a good word for all desert flora—but not for cholla.

mingbird, common raven, cactus wren, black-throated sparrow. Others that might be seen are the zebra-tailed lizard, iguana, and the desert tortoise.

DESERT DRY WOODLAND

Dry, sandy wash communities are found throughout the preserve, wherever water carves its way after a thunderstorm or extended rainy period. Usually found in valleys beneath the mountains, these dry drainage areas quickly fill with an enormous volume of water following storms. These flash floods carry boulders, rocks, shrubs, and any other debris that cross their course.

Desert willows, with their long taproots that seek a permanent water supply, are common along washes. Their pink-lined trumpet-shaped flowers, long pods and slender leaves makes them easily identifiable.

Other plants that grow along drainage washes include mesquite and cat's claw, two related species that bloom with yellow flowers. Desert holly, desert almond and several wildflower species flourish here after winter rains.

Animals include many of the same dwellers found in other desert communities: jackrabbit, desert cottontail, ground squirrel, desert wood rat, cactus mouse, several birds, lizards, sidewinder and desert tortoise.

PINYON-JUNIPER WOODLAND

This community is found in desert mountains between 3,500 and 6,000 feet in elevation. In Mojave National Preserve, pinyon-juniper woodlands can be explored in the New York, Providence and Ivanpah ranges, as well as Clark Mountain.

Visit this pinyon-juniper woodland in the Granite Mountains.

Higher elevations, cooler temperatures and greater amounts of moisture than occur in low-lying valleys allow the growth of pinyon pine, California and Utah juniper and scrub oak. Other species typically found include black bush, box thorn, Mojave yucca, silver cholla and desert bunch grass.

Coyote, jackrabbit, California ground squirrel, pocket gopher and pinon mouse inhabit the woodland community, as do a number of birds, including the woodpecker, pinon jay, rock wren, black-throated gray warbler and gray vireo.

> The pine nuts belong to the mountain
> We ask the mountain that we may have of its pine nuts.
> We would eat.
> —Piute Pine Nut Prayer

RIPARIAN WOODLANDS AND MARSHES

Found along streams such as Piute Creek and along the Mojave River in Afton Canyon and near Camp Cady, this community's year-round water supply supports trees such as cottonwood, willow and mesquite. These native species, however, are threatened by the growth of the nonnative tamarisk, which was introduced to the area from the Mediterranean more than 100 years ago. The invasive tamarisk, also called salt cedar, consumes great amounts of water, and tends to choke out the other

The invasive tamarisk threatens to choke out native species.

trees. Efforts to remove the tamarisk must be very aggressive to be effective; chain saws and strong herbicides are required. Each year volunteer workers spend countless hours clearing riparian areas of the tenacious invader.

Streamside communities frequently attract large bird populations, and the seasonal habitation of migratory species. Many other desert dwellers seek water in riparian communities, most spectacular of which is the bighorn sheep, which are known to frequent Afton Canyon in the dark and quiet hours.

THE DESERT IN BLOOM

Wildflower displays are especially delightful in the desert. Brightly colored blossoms contrast vibrantly with the neutral-hued desert environment. But wildflowers bloom only when conditions allow. There must be plenty of evenly spaced winter precipitation, and warmth, but not too much heat in the spring. Kelso Dunes, Ivanpah Valley and the Cadiz Dunes (just south of Mojave), are three areas where wildflowers can be expected when the conditions are right.

Coreopsis, encelia, desert primrose, desert verbena and the blooms of the Mohave mound cactus are just a few of the more common Mojave wildflowers.

The plants and animals of the desert, confronted continually with the harshness of their environment, have made remarkable adaptations in order to survive. Desert visitors can help ensure their survival by enjoying, observing and photographing the numerous species, but not disturbing them in any way.

MOJAVE WILDLIFE

While hundreds of animal species inhabit the desert, you're likely to see only a few. You're almost guaranteed to spot jackrabbits and range cattle, ravens and an assortment of lizards and birds; you may even spot a coyote near dusk. But you may travel in this arid land for years before spotting a bighorn sheep or desert tortoise. The animals are there, but they tend to be quite reclusive.

Bighorn Sheep

The desert bighorn sheep is one of the most majestic, and easily the most distinct animal to roam the Mojave.

They are magnificent creatures, shy and usually hidden from sight. They live primarily on rugged mountain peaks, venturing to lowlands only to water occasionally.

Bighorns were frequently depicted in Native American petroglyphs and pictographs; capturing one on film is a special experience indeed for amateur and professional photographers.

Because the sheep roam areas far removed from people, sighting one of them is an experience usually reserved only for those hikers willing to climb high into

Mojave's mountain ranges. Often the "photo opportunity" is a fleeting one; bighorns can scramble over tough terrain with amazing speed.

Both males and females grow horns; however, it's the truly big curled horns of the males that earned bighorns their name. A mature curl takes seven to eight years to grow, and can measure 30 inches from base to tip.

While the animal's massive horns give *Ovis Canadensis* its regal appearance, it's the distinct configuration of the sheep's stomach that enables it to survive in a very harsh environment. Bighorns are able to browse on some of the desert's driest, hardest and most nutrient-deficient plants. Still, they're able to thrive on such a diet thanks to a complex nine-stage digestive system allowing them to extract a maximum of nutrients from marginal food sources.

Just as the sheep have adapted to a limited food supply, they've also adapted to an even more limited water supply. In fact, during the "green months" of winter, the sheep get all the water they need from available vegetation. During the summer, bighorns visit waterholes every couple days. By making only brief and infrequent visits to waterholes, bighorns minimize their exposure to lurking predators.

The preserve's bighorn population is estimated at between 700 and 1,000 animals.

Bighorns live 10 to 15 years. Females (ewes) weigh 75 to 130 pounds, while males (rams) tip the scale at about double that—140 to 220 pounds or more. Ewes typically first breed at about 2½ years old and usually deliver one lamb (occasionally two) in late spring, following a six-month long gestation period.

The winter of 1988 was the first time in 114 years that hunting of bighorn sheep was authorized and legal in California. A national preserve, unlike a national park, allows hunting, so hunting for bighorn sheep has continued, even after the National Park Service began administering Mojave. The California Department of Fish and Game sold a hunting permit for $100,000 in 1993, one for $150,000 in 1998.

Somewhat ironically, the same agency that has authorized hunting of the rare bighorn sheep is also the agency charged with its protection and observation. Throughout the year, DFG wardens construct watering holes in remote places for the large animals and carefully monitor their behavior, migration routes and numbers.

Tortoises

Warm spring weather brings hibernating tortoises out of their winter burrows, just in time to munch on wildflowers in bloom. These slow-moving, prehistoric-looking creatures have long been a favorite animal of children and their parents as well. Prime springtime viewing areas of desert tortoises include Ivanpah and Fenner Valleys. Kelbaker Road, from Baker to Kelso, is an-

This visitor knows to observe the desert tortoise from a respectful distance. Look, but don't touch.

other good place to see them; during the spring months, drive this road with special care for the safety of the tortoises.

If you spot one of these creatures, do not disturb it. Sit quietly and observe it, photograph it, record notes about it, but don't touch it, pick it up or bother it in any way.

The California Desert Tortoise is the state official reptile, fully protected by state and federal laws. Unfortunately, the tortoise's habitat — and population — have shrunk alarmingly in recent years.

In July of 1989, the U.S. Fish and Wildlife Service, in a rare emergency move, designated the desert tortoise as an endangered species. Citing evidence that the population of the reptile has declined up to sixty percent in some areas of the California desert, the agency agreed with several environmental groups working to protect the desert tortoise.

Human activities are largely the cause for the demise of the desert tortoise. Off-road vehicles are a major factor; not only do they occasionally run over the animals, but they crush their burrows and compact the earth. Some unconscionable individuals have actually used the slow-moving tortoises for target practice—hardly a sporting or defensible undertaking.

The increasing raven population has also been blamed for the decline of the tortoise. The clever birds prey on tortoises and easily pick off the near-defenseless, lumbering creatures, especially the young. The problem has reached such levels that officials have considered shooting or poisoning the ravens to bring their numbers under control.

In recent years, the tortoise population, now listed as a "threatened" species, has faced yet another threat—a respiratory virus that was once virtually unknown in the wild. They appear to have contracted the deadly virus from tortoises that were once kept as pets, then re-released into the wild. Today, the survival of these ancient animals, which have been called "living fossils," depends on both human intervention and simply giving them a relatively undisturbed environment in which to live.

Burros

Scores of burros were first brought to the desert a century ago by prospectors who loaded them up with supplies and headed west. The animals proved to be remarkably well-adapted to the climate and terrain; the descendants of those Gold Rush pack animals now number into several thousand feral animals who forage throughout the American desert.

Although we might enjoy a warm, fuzzy image of the wild burro, the truth is that the animal causes considerable damage to the environment. Mojave National Preserve provides these feral animals with many tasty treats. They destroy ground cover that protects many animals from predators and intense sunlight, and they trample the

ground-and any unfortunate little animals that may get in their way.

National Park Service policy mandates that land under its stewardship be returned to a naturally functioning ecosystem; this strict environmental guideline means all burros must be removed from Mojave National Preserve.

The burro is a descendant of the Nubian and Somalian wild ass (*Equus asinus* to be exact), and was domesticated in Africa some 5,000 years ago. Nineteenth-century prospectors used burros to help them work desert diggings through the American Southwest, and usually turned the animals loose after completing their mining activity. Burros were used in the early years of the twentieth century, too, until miners replaced their beasts of burden with motorized vehicles.

The burro is remarkably adaptable to life in the Mojave Desert. Adequate forage in the form of grasses, plants and flowers keeps them fed, and remote springs and water sources slake their thirst. In more recent years, burros have discovered Mojave's strategically placed wildlife guzzlers—intended to aid bighorn sheep.

Many of the animals average a healthy 400 to 450 pounds while a few of the biggest burros weigh in at more than 600 pounds.

Burros are voracious and not-very-picky eaters and devour vegetation that's vital to the California desert tortoise. Burros have a tendency to pick clean an area of its plant diversity, leaving behind only the woodiest of shrubs.

The National Park Service's Burro Removal Program has been quite an undertaking. Helicopters were used to count the animals, which were "shot" with paint-balls in order to mark them. Burros are often captured when they wander through one-way gates into corrals in search of water.

Not only are burros highly adaptable and long-lived (up to 40 years), they're extremely fertile and, if left alone to reproduce, can increase their population by as much as 25 percent a year. Thus, burro relocators will have to capture some 3,000 animals—nearly twice the number of burros roaming the preserve when the removal program began.

Until all the burros are removed from the park, visitors will likely spot burro hoof prints and droppings along many park trails. Often visitors are surprised to spot burros in what seem to be the most inhospitable parts of the preserve. Along Kelbaker Road, for example, keen-eyed travelers may spot burros on the edge of the lava beds and high in the Granite Mountains—difficult terrain to be sure!

While burro removal from national park land (Grand Canyon National Park, Death Valley National Park, etc.) has been a common practice for decades, Mojave National Preserve has pioneered some innovative placement programs.

Wranglers and Park Rangers are removing all burros from Mojave.

The park service has partnered with contract wranglers who offer some of the burros for adoption to rural families.

In 1998, Mojave National Preserve Superintendent Mary Martin signed an agreement with noted animal rights activist Cleveland Amory and his Fund for Animals organization. Under the landmark agreement, completed shortly before Amory's death, captured burros will be sent to the Fund for Animals' Black Beauty Ranch in Texas to live out their days.

Reptiles

Many species of lizards live in the preserve, including the zebratail, whiptail, leopard and collared lizard. Dune-dwelling fringe-toed lizards are a strange sight as they scoot over the sand on their hind legs, then dive into a dune and "swim" below the sand. The two-foot-long, generally nocturnal Gila monster is well known but infrequently observed in the preserve.

Second in size only to the Gila monster, the chuckwalla is found on many a rocky slope. *Sauromalu obis* ("fat bad lizard" by its Latin name) looks clumsy but it can scale a creosote bush and shake down the blossoms, which it eats. When frightened, the chuckwalla can puff out its loose skin and become immovably wedged in a rocky crevice.

Researchers say the large dominant males, called tyrants, gather harems and fiercely fend off rivals. Mating behavior among the chuckwalla has been described as erotic: females arouse males by rubbing and licking them.

Mojave's most commonly sighted snake is the red racer, as fast as its name suggests-or at least the fastest snake in this desert. The six-foot-long snake can race along at seven miles per hour. While not poisonous, the snake is known for its nasty temper and can bite.

The desert rosy boa, identified by three broad stripes down its back, is found near springs, creeks and other (relatively) wetter parts of the preserve. While a member of the boa family of Amazon fame, it reaches but a fraction of the size of its tropical cousins—only two to three feet long.

The gopher snake, with coloration and patterning resembling that of a rattler, is found throughout the preserve. This resemblance to the rattler, and the fact that they're among the most easily handled and captured of snakes, means unthinking desert travelers often harm or kill them. Gopher snakes are not poisonous and kill their prey (rodents, rabbits, lizards) by constriction.

The Mojave Desert sidewinder's means of locomotion is unique to say the least. Unlike snakes that use their bottom scales to crawl along, the sidewinder tosses its head forward; then, using its head as an anchor, it pulls the rest of itself along. This style of travel is particularly effective in sandy areas of the preserve such as Kelso Dunes.

In the unlikely event that you spot a snake in Mojave, simply leave it alone.

The poisonous Mojave rattlesnake is regarded as one of the most dangerous rattlers in the Mojave Desert. It generally inhabits the creosote bush community at an elevation of 2,000 to 4,000 feet. With coloring ranging from green-gray to yellowish hues, and with white-edged diamond shapes along its back, the Mojave rattlesnake resembles the diamondback rattlesnake.

3

Mojave History

The land we now call Mojave National Preserve has long been both a home and a gateway to the Far West. During the last century, however, it has also been viewed as a place that offers enough natural resources to support a specialized way of life. More recently, the view of the desert has been enlarged to one of a playground where cramped city dwellers can pursue recreational activities in wide-open spaces. Accompanying and influencing these changing perceptions of our citizenry's relationship with the desert has been a growing controversy over which governmental agencies can best supervise, preserve and protect this land, and the activities it supports.

EARLIEST HABITATION

During the Pleistocene Epoch, less than a half-million years ago, much of the area was filled with the waters of Lake Manix, which supported not only abundant wildlife and vegetation, but a significant human habitation as well.

Archeologists disagree about the time of human habitation; one school of thought refers to "early arrivals," the other to "late arrivals." Much of the controversy stems from the work of Dr. Louis S.B. Leakey, who supervised the massive excavation now called the Calico Early Man Site. The work, which began in 1964, was funded by the National Geographic Society. More than 11,000 artifacts have been found here in the alluvial material from the shores of ancient Lake Manix. Leakey determined them to be 200,000 years old. Virtually all other scientists disagree with this determination and estimate that the earliest people first inhabited this area some 10,000 to 12,000 years ago.

Although no human remains of Early Man have been recovered from the Calico site, the chipped stone tools found appear to be evidence of the oldest human habitation in the Americas. To the average visitor to the site, however, whether the first habitation occurred 10,000 or 200,000 years ago hardly matters; the fact is, human beings have lived here a very long time, a period unimaginable to most of us.

Ancient peoples, who lived here up to

Chumehuevi, native people of the California desert.

about 11,000 years ago, left flaked and fluted stone artifacts and throwing sticks. Evidence of more recent dwellers, dated to about 200 years ago, can be seen in other cultural artifacts including arrow points, mortars and pestles, pottery, petroglyphs and cave dwellings. Shells found in caves indicate that desert dwellers were engaged in trade with coastal natives; evidence of turquoise mining near Clark Mountain and pottery shards found throughout the East Mojave lead archeologists and anthropologists to surmise that Pueblos from the north and east regularly visited this area to mine and trade. The routes followed by these travelers later became major transportation routes through the desert.

Even as the area's weather changed and became more arid, and the water supply largely dried up, the Mojave River continued to flow year-round in many areas of this desert. This availability of water ensured that humans could continue to inhabit the area.

The native people of Mojave—Piutes, Mojave and Chemehuevi—were well-adapted to their environment and managed to flourish in what we today consider a most inhospitable environment. They ate what was available: mesquite, prickly pear, tule roots and roasted agave blooms. They trapped and hunted deer and bighorn sheep, rodents, snakes, and birds in the New York and Providence Mountains. They used natural materials to craft what they needed —baskets from roots and willows, metates and mortars from stones for food preparation, needles and drills out of bones. They sought shelter where they found it; the Chemehuevi used the caves in the Provi-

Some Mojave tribal groups practiced irrigation along the Colorado River.

dence Mountains—among them the present-day Mitchell Caverns—for more than 500 years.

Although one would suppose that these nomadic hunter-gatherers had little leisure time, anthropologists believe that they did enjoy a rich oral tradition of storytelling and participated in many games. They engaged in ceremonial activities, often tied to the change of seasons, and fashioned petroglyphs—the meaning of which is still unclear. These artifacts can still be seen throughout the area, silent indicators of cultures very different from our own.

PALEONTOLOGICAL RESOURCES

No large-scale, systematic archeological work has been conducted in Mojave National Preserve, though sites discovered thus far are quite intriguing to scientists. Prehistoric villages with rock shelters, petroglyphs, and quarries have been found in the Providence Mountains; rock shelters and pictographs in the Granite Mountains; petroglyphs in the Woods Mountains, Cinder Cones and Lanfair Valley.

Other discoveries range from tool-making sites on Pleistocene-era lakeshores to campsites and petroglyphs found along ancient trails that led from the Colorado River to the Pacific coast.

Mojave's fossil record is nearly as extensive (and complex!) as its geological record. Fossil remains help scientists (1) date corresponding geological features, (2) trace the

Ancient rocks tell the story of Mojave's earliest inhabitants.

evolutionary paths of plants and animals, and (3) illustrate the area's many environmental changes.

Some of Mojaves paleontological highlights include:

• The world's oldest mitosing cells, nearly a billion years old, are preserved in silica in the Beck Spring Formation.

• Significant Cambrian (600 million years ago) trilobite and invertebrate fossils typical of marine life when the area was covered by shallow seas

• Large deposits of such fossils as rhinoceros and camel, as well as plants and bird tracks in several preserve locales including Lanfair Valley and the Castle Mountains.

SPANISH EXPLORATION

Travel through the desert, although it posed many hardships and challenges to early explorers, was preferable to traveling through the mountains that served as a more formidable barrier to westward movement.

On his journey to the coast from what is now known as the Gila Valley in Arizona, Spanish explorer/Franciscan priest, Father Francisco Garcés began his travel through Mojave in 1776. Accompanied by three Mohave Indians, Fr. Garcés followed the Old Mojave Trail, from Piute Springs through the New York Mountains, over the Providence Mountains, Kelso Dunes and Soda Lake. He named the lake Arroyo de los Martires (River of the Martyrs). He also

Father Francisco Garcés passed through Mojave in 1776. He was killed five years later by the Yumas.

Explorer John C. Frémont and his men worked up an "intolerable thirst" when crossing Mojave.

journeyed through Afton Canyon, which he called Sierra Pinta for the streaks of minerals that colored the canyon.

The natives not only led the friar along the route, but provided him with supplies and gifts. He described them as ". . . very quiet and inoffensive, and they hear with attention that which is told them of God."

The founding of the missions in California led to increased travel across the desert, and the establishment of the Spanish Trail—part of which became known as the Mojave Road—as the favored route west.

AMERICANS PUSH WEST

In 1826, Jedediah Strong Smith, one of the new breed of adventurous American fur trappers, followed the Colorado River from the north, then across the Mojave, along Garcés' route. Other notable explorers who traveled through the Mojave include Kit Carson and John C. Frémont.

Frémont, who followed the Old Mojave Road in the 1840s, called it "the roughest and rockiest road we had ever seen." He continued: "Travellers through countries affording water and timber can have no conception of our intolerable thirst while journeying over the hot yellow sands of this elevated country, where the heated air seems to be entirely deprived of moisture."

During the days when Manifest Destiny was the operating philosophy, America's western wilderness was seen as something to be conquered, settled and tamed. Forests

"American Graffiti" left behind by 19th century travelers on the old Mojave Road.

were leveled, prairies were planted and the land was seen as virgin territory awaiting the hand of man.

The open space and barrenness of the desert was viewed by overland travelers as an obstacle to life itself; they hardly considered settling in such an environment. All they wanted to do was get through it as quickly and safely as possible. Fearing not only the harsh, unfamiliar land, but the Indians who lived there, travel through the desert was considered one of the most trying ordeals of the entire journey.

Although the native population eyed the intruders on their land as warily as the pioneers regarded them, their numbers soon declined, and their land was gradually lost as the newcomers settled in. As was the case throughout the West, cowboy-and-Indian stories were more than the stuff of legend; there were many fierce clashes between the native people and white travelers in this desert.

Hike to the isolated ruins of Fort Piute and travel back in time.

Camp Ibis, located in Mojave, was the site of military maneuvers, as were many other desert locales.

MILITARY THEN AND NOW

Because wagon trains and stage coaches were frequently attacked along the Old Mojave Road, the United States government established a number of army outposts. Fort Piute, Camp Rock Springs and Camp Cady were built in the 1860s to house the soldiers and escorts assigned to accompany and protect immigrants and mail carriers. These tiny camps, situated in such lonely territory, were never staffed by more than a few soldiers at a time; desertion and understaffing were always problems at the Mojave desert forts.

By the late 1860s, the native populations were decimated by war, disease and displacement to reservations. With their superior firepower, technology and the power of law on their side, the newcomers simply overcame the resistance of the native people and claimed control of the land. As the natives were subdued, the need for military outposts was lessened, and all of them were abandoned in just a decade. They stand in ruins to this day.

During the late 1890s and early years of the twentieth century, California and U.S. geologists studied the mineral exploitation potential of what is now Mojave National Preserve. The U.S. Geological Survey produced the first reliable topographic maps of the region.

In 1909, the agency published a guide to the "watering places" that provided crucial directions and maps about the location of springs and artesian water sources for the use of travelers and settlers.

The open land of the desert has continued to appeal to military planners. In the 1940s, General George S. Patton trained World War II troops in war games conducted throughout the California Desert; evidence of the Iron Mountain Camp (located near Joshua Tree National Park), tank tracks and other scars on the land—-remain distinct many decades later. In the early 1960s,

Operation Desert Strike was conducted in the eastern Mojave. One hundred thousand men, and a massive amount of equipment, spent a month training near Fort Piute. A marker on U.S. 95 pays tribute to the operation.

Calling the 1964 war games an example of "very grave destruction," Edmund C. Jaeger observed, "It appears that little if any thought was given to the preservation of the natural amenities of this magnificent sweep of fragile desert. Not in a hundred years can the damage be repaired by nature even if no further exercises take place."

His comments characterize the prevailing position in opposition to the military's use of the desert. While branches of the military continue to view the desert as a vast expanse of open land especially well-suited to their training exercises, others see it as a unique and fragile ecosystem that

Tank in a live-fire war game.

may be forever damaged by high-impact activities.

The military's use of the desert is not limited to the land itself. The airspace above Mojave National Preserve is considered prime for testing and training flights for exotic supersonic jets, the Stealth bomber, for example. Unsuspecting drivers or hikers are frequently surprised when they hear the sound of fast-moving military jets swooping low overhead.

MINING

Gold Rush fever of the 1800s prompted men to look at the land not only for the crops it might support, but for what riches lay beneath the soil. Since the desert was so obviously lacking in resources to support life,

it stood to reason to many that it must be hiding much good deep below. Early twentieth-century author and California booster George Wharton James expressed the prevailing sentiment of his time when he wrote: "A place which is obviously so cursed that nothing will grow on it must have been created by the Lord of all things for some purpose and the only purpose it could possibly have was to carry minerals hidden somewhere below its forbidden surface."

One mode of hauling ore—more powerful than a 20-mule team, circa 1887.

Because Mojave has such a varied geology you might expect a wide variety of mineral resources—and truly an impressive array of minerals has been discovered. Gold, silver, zinc, iron ore and copper are among the more common metallic elements that have been successfully mined. Discoveries of these elements led to the establishment of many mining camp towns in this desert. Despite the harshness of the land and the extreme climate, the towns of Ivanpah, Hart and Vanderbilt sprang up to serve the needs of the miners. In the pages of this guide, and during your travels through the preserve, you'll learn more about these one-time boomtowns.

In 1863, prospectors discovered silver near Rock Springs in the present Mojave National Preserve. Mining camps sprang up overnight in the Providence Mountains, New York Mountains, and elsewhere, but the primary settlement remained at Rock Springs, where the area's first post office was established in 1866.

More silver was discovered south of Clark Mountain in 1869, prompting the establishment of Ivanpah, where much of Mojave's mining was centered during the 1870s. Ivanpah prospectors discovered the rich Bonanza King silver mine on the eastern slopes of the Providence Mountains in 1883.

Gold mining predominated in the 1890s, due to the widespread use of cyanide used to extract gold from ore; this process allowed prospectors to return to old, formerly unprofitable mines to rework the diggings. Other mining ventures of this era included development of copper, lead and silver deposits in the New York Mountains.

During the early 1900s, gold was discovered in the Castle Mountains, copper on Clark Mountain, zinc and silver at Mid Hills. Sporadic mining efforts continued through the decades, but it was not until World War II that another mining boom occurred in the eastern Mojave.

During the 1940s, Kaiser Steel Company established the Vulcan Iron Ore Mine in the Providence Mountains. The successful mine created a short-lived boom in the town of Kelso, where most of the miners lived with their families. By the end of the decade, the mine shut down, and the population of Kelso declined from a high of 1,500 down to just a few hundred.

Abandoned mining sites honeycomb many of the mountains throughout the preserve, and can still be found by hikers and explorers.

(Use great care around such sites; it's not safe to enter them.)

Over the years, as human use of Mojave has changed, so too has the prevailing land ethic. What was once seen as digging and scratching at the earth now looks like the scarring and misuse of a fragile land. Today, while there are several responsible mining operations unearthing necessary minerals for the public good, there are also far too many shoddy operations—many based on bogus claims—that are simply ecologically as well as economically indefensible. These latter claims, conservationists say, must go.

Central to the mining issue is the General Mining Law of 1872, which allows individuals to stake a claim on the land after a valuable mineral deposit has been discovered. These claims are purchased for little money and require few improvements on the land in order to maintain them or a

small fee. Claims can be purchased, willed or inherited. Although the federal government is required to put each claim to a "prudent man and marketability test," many questionable mining claims go unchallenged year after year.

The image of the grizzled old miner staking his claim, and scratching out a living on the earth is romantic and quite appealing. But mining in the desert is no longer done by a lone individual armed with a pick-axe and shovel. It's conducted by major mining corporations which use sophisticated methods to extract minerals from the ground.

The Mountain Pass area, near Clark Mountain, contains a rich mine of the rare earth element bastnasite, along with other rare earths with the science fiction sounding names of cerium, lanthanum and neodymium. These rare earth minerals are used in research related to the high-tech field of superconductivity, along with petroleum-processing, metallurgical and glass-making applications.

"What are cows doing out here?" visitors wonder.

RANCHING

"What are they doing out here?" visitors ask when they see forlorn cows standing in the meager shade of a Joshua tree.

Many a dirt road drive through the preserve results in an encounter with range cattle. Although this a land of sparse vegetation, cattle ranching has long been considered a way of life here.

Beginning in the 1860s, ranchers shadowed miners in the eastern Mojave; they raised cattle to supply neighboring mining camps. Business was often good-for as long as the local mine produced.

In 1894, the Rock Springs Land & Cattle Company consolidated several early ranches in the present preserve and over into southern Nevada. By 1920, the ranch boasted 10,000 head of cattle spread out over more than a million acres. From 1927 until 1988, OX Cattle Company, an offshoot of the original Rock Springs outfit, was the largest ranching operation in Mojave.

Fewer than a half-dozen individuals ranch here today; it's become an unprofitable and difficult way of life. One management difference between a national park and a national preserve is the presence of

One of the few differences between a national park and preserve: some ranching is permitted in Mojave National Preserve.

grazing animals. From the Colton Hills to Valley Wells, and from Gold Valley to the Granite Mountains, visitors might spot bovines in the brush.

By law, the ranchers' grazing allotments may not exceed levels allowed in 1994 when the preserve was established.

The preserve would seem an ideal area for implementation of an innovative federal program that enables conservation organizations to purchase grazing rights from willing sellers and "retire" them. This program would compensate ranchers for the loss of grazing land, and allow grazed land to return to its natural state.

RAILROAD

The coming of the railroad to the desert linked the eastern Mojave to the rest of the world, making settlement attractive, and business more profitable.

The mostly small, private railroad lines were established by wealthy industrialists who envisioned increasing their fortunes by transporting desert riches to major shipping

Although it was intended to run from Nevada to the Pacific, the closest the T&T got to a water source was Broad Dry Lake.

points. Francis Marion "Borax" Smith constructed the Tidewater and Tonopah line to service his borax mine in the Death Valley area.

The Nevada Southern Railroad operated from 1893 until 1923. It served the tiny towns of Goffs and Lanfair, Barnwell and Vontrigger. Homesteaders, ranchers and miners who settled in the area were able to ship their supplies, cattle and ores on the line. The railroad declined due to a combination of factors: damage to the lines from shifting sands, flash flooding and disuse as the area's population dwindled.

The Union Pacific, which came to the east Mojave during World War I, frequently runs trains on tracks through the preserve; freight lines rumble through regularly, as

Railroads are not just a nostalgic reminder of days gone by; many lines are still in service.

well as a single passenger train (with intermittent service) from Los Angeles to Las Vegas daily. Taking the train through the desert allows passengers to view parts of Mojave National Preserve inaccessible by motor vehicle. And no one can deny the romance of the rails. As the song goes, "There's something about a train."

RECREATION

The desert, first in the hearts of the many who love it, was the last of the state's regions to be preserved. Early conservationists first worked to preserve the glorious mountains and forests; next came the coast and coastal mountains. And finally, the desert.

The desert's recreation potential followed a similar pattern. First Californians and visitors from elsewhere took to the mountains, then the seashore, lastly to the desert. At the beginning of the twentieth century, resorts and recreation of all sorts were well established in the state's alpine and coastal regions, but only a few hardy prospectors roamed the desert.

It wasn't until the 1920s and the development of (somewhat) dependable autos that Americans began discovering the Mojave Desert. Today the desert provides open spaces, solitude and quiet—all of which are in short supply in congested urban areas.

City dwellers looking for adventure have found it in various forms in the desert—

some which have virtually no impact on the environment, others that have alarmingly destructive consequences. Hiking, photography, painting, bird-watching, astronomy, and other low-impact activities allow desert visitors to enjoy the environment while preserving its integrity for years to come.

The same cannot be said, however, for those who engage in activities such as riding off-road vehicles irresponsibly, shooting and committing acts of vandalism. While off-road riding in the preserve is strictly prohibited by law, many choose to ignore the rules, and tear up land in the process. Off-highway vehicles scar the fragile desert land, and cause extensive damage to plants and animals that inhabit it

Many of the prime spots in the preserve are accessible only by dirt road; there's no question that four-wheel drive vehicles are well-suited to desert travel. Those who responsibly tour into the heart of the desert on dirt roads (including the historic Mojave Road) may be delighted with the richness of the experience.

But the desert demands a closer look. To appreciate fully Mojave's beauty requires a bit of walking-a stroll through a devil's garden of cactus, a hike up the Kelso Dunes, the trek to the top of a desert peak. Without a doubt, Mojave is most enticing when approached on foot.

4

Mojave National Preserve: Yesterday and Today

Mojave National Preserve (and all other national park land) was established to preserve outstanding natural, cultural, and scenic resources while providing for scientific, educational, and recreational interests.

As the National Park Service sees it, Mojave National Preserve has three important purposes: (1) Preserve and protect the natural and scenic resources of the Mojave Desert, including transitional elements of the Sonoran and Great Basin deserts; (2) Preserve and protect cultural resources representing human use associated with Native American cultures and westward expansion; (3) Provide opportunities for compatible outdoor recreation and promote understanding and appreciation of the California desert.

The National Park Service's Mojave mission is more conservationist-oriented than that of earlier official stewards of this land. When East Mojave National Scenic Area was established in 1980 it was placed under the administration of the Bureau of Land Management, part of the U.S. Department of the Interior. The BLM was assigned the task of protecting the scenic, cultural and recreational features of 1.5 million acres of desert, while also overseeing mining, ranching and off-highway vehicle use.

Mojave was first managed by the U.S. Bureau of Land Management.

The U.S. Bureau of Land Management came into being in 1946 when the General Land Office (often referred to as "the government's real estate agent") and the U.S. Grazing Service were combined into a single agency. During the Bureau's early years, desert administrators and their counterparts throughout the West operated under confusing and sometimes conflicting federal mandates.

Passage of the Federal Land Policy Management Act (FLPMA) of 1976 helped nudge the BLM into more modern ways of managing its vast holdings of government land. "Flipma," as it's usually referred to, provided, among other things, that: (1) Outdoor recreation be a principal or major use of public lands; (2) BLM evaluate all public lands for their wilderness values and make recommendations to Congress of Wilderness Area designation; (3) BLM manage established wilderness areas under the provisions of the Wilderness Act of 1964; (4) BLM be empowered to have a program of law enforcement and a ranger force to patrol its most environmentally sensitive properties. (BLM's very first rangers were assigned to the California desert.)

Long before the federal government enacted its many Acts and Plans, Mojave was known to possess unusual combinations of plants and animals, striking geology and scenery, and a great potential for recreation. However, it was not until the whole California desert began to be (re)evaluated by the federal government during the 1970s that the desert in general, and the Mojave in particular, began receiving the attention—and protection—it had long deserved.

The Bureau began operating its Scenic Area under the framework of its California Desert Conservation Area Plan. This plan, which cost $8 million, was formulated after a four-year study. The BLM gathered an astonishing 40,000 public responses for its plan, believed to be the largest regional planning effort ever attempted in the United States.

BLM's Desert Plan was gigantic in scope, as was the land it covered—25 million acres of California desert. When BLM's long-awaited Desert Plan was completed, a *Los Angeles Times* editorial, perhaps summing up the mood of many citizens who contributed to the grueling planning process, stated: "The plan appears to protect the interests of preservationists while recognizing the needs of miners, ranchers and utility companies. It is a balanced plan no group will be entirely happy with and that's a good sign."

Particularly unhappy with the plan and BLM's interpretation of its mandate were environmentalists who claimed that the agency, wedded by law to its multiple use doctrine, had over-emphasized commodity production and utilitarian use over wilderness preservation and wildlife management. Critics claimed that Congress gave BLM an impossible task—a balancing act impossible to perform.

To the agency's critics, the most glaring example of mismanagement of fragile desert resources was its supervision of off-highway vehicle use. The Barstow to Las Vegas motorcycle races through Mojave were particularly upsetting to conservationists.

Until halted in 1989, the B-V race was an extremely emotional issue for both sides. (Unfortunately for the public's awareness of the desert, race day seemed to be the only day that the major media ventured anywhere near this desert.)

The desert debate, which had focused on mining, OHV use and the quantity of land that the BLM had proposed in its plans to set aside as wilderness, heated up

Sen. Alan Cranston:
the consummate
politician with the
instincts of a
conservationist.

sharply in 1987 when California Senator Alan Cranston introduced his California Desert Protection Act to Congress. The far-reaching bill attempted to create three new national parks: two were "upgrades" of Joshua Tree and Death Valley national monuments, while the third proposed a Mojave National Park. The latter park was to be formed largely from land included within the bounds of BLM's East Mojave National Scenic Area.

Senator Cranston and many in the environmental community, including the Sierra Club and the California Desert Protection League, believed that only National Park Service management could adequately protect these desert lands. "The biggest reason [for Mojave National Park]," stated Cranston, "is that the desert is being scarred forever, its natural state destroyed by off-road vehicles that are not controlled adequately as to where they can go, and by those who seek development."

Other conservationists at the time figured that Mojave could be managed in a more park-like manner without actually stripping the BLM of the land and transferring it to the National Park Service. They contended that the BLM was financially hamstrung from implementing its desert plans; with more money and more manpower, the agency would be a more vigilant guardian of the Mojave.

The BLM itself claimed that it had shed much of its commodity development orientation and was a true resource management agency. Many BLM rangers and administrators insisted that their agency gave the East Mojave top priority; the National Park Service would adjudge Mojave National Park a very low priority, they argued.

After the California Desert Bill was first introduced in 1987, it was modified and reintroduced again and again over the years. Rep. Mel Levine introduced similar legislation in the U.S. House of Representatives.

Sign of the times: Graphic opposition to Sen. Cranston's desert protection legislation.

To say that legislation proposing Mojave National Park created a lot of controversy in these parts is like saying the desert has a lot of sand. Both sides produced mountains of literature and hours of videotape supporting their positions on everything from the effects of off-highway vehicle noise on the kangaroo rat's hearing to the use of cyanide in gold mining.

Over the years the debate assumed several dimensions—economic, aesthetic, moral, political, even philosophical. Elden Hughes, chairman of the California Desert Protection League, repeatedly stated that the desert was more than an issue to him— it was a passion. This Sierra Club activist and self-proclaimed desert rat spent—and still spends—most of his spare time in the desert photographing everything from grand landscapes to rare flowers, and exploring places virtually unknown to even those familiar with the Mojave. "I've trav-

Desert protection advocate Elden Hughes: the consummate conservationist with the instincts of a politician.

eled this desert all my life," he stated. "It's park quality, and the Park Service is best able to protect it."

Soon after taking office, California Senator Dianne Feinstein introduced the California Desert Protection Act of 1993. Like the Senator Cranston-sponsored bills before it, the legislation was designed to create national parks of Death Valley and Joshua Tree national monuments, as well as establish a new Mojave National Park. The bill called for a 1.5-million acre park, with about half that acreage set aside in wilderness areas. The bill, boosted by California's outspoken Senator Barbara Boxer, passed in November 1994, but at the last minute anti-park legislators succeeded in altering Mojave's status from a park to preserve, thus retaining certain forms of hunting, grazing and mining activity.

Today park officials and the public alike recognize Mojave National Preserve as the best place to experience the extensive variety of habitats, species, and landforms unique to the Mojave Desert.

In 1998, the National Park Service completed the first draft of its General Management Plan. The document, created with much public input, urges strong measures for protection of the preserve's resources while advocating increased interpretive efforts and visitor services.

Part II

Traveling to Mojave National Preserve

Desert Travel

Many notable travelers have journeyed through the hot white heart of the Mojave since Father Francisco Garcés first passed this way in 1776. Other early Mojave explorers include Jedediah Smith, Kit Carson, and John C. Frémont. They had little idea of what to expect during their desert crossing. Traveling without detailed maps, high-tech equipment, or freeze-dried foods, they still managed to make the overland trek toward the coast.

Today, we enjoy the benefit of all sorts of undreamed-of modern accoutrements, making desert journeys more comfortable than they were in days past. But the most important aids to desert travel remain as

The Automobile Club of Southern California was instrumental in mapping, signing, and improving desert roads.

simple as they were 200 years ago—common sense, advance planning and packing the right supplies.

PLANNING AHEAD

Individuals accustomed to spending their days in air-conditioned comfort are in for a surprise when they venture into the desert. It's a harsh environment that demands adaptation by inhabitants and visitors alike. Daily extremes of hot and cold are the norm; a 100-degree day can become a 50-degree night. It's important to be prepared—not simply for comfort, but for survival.

The unforgiving desert does not allow visitors to make many mistakes. Those ill-prepared may be unable to deal with threatening situations. Desert dangers are real, and using common sense is essential.

Planning ahead is the first rule of desert travel. Study maps and know where you're going. Become informed about weather patterns, and know what temperatures and climatic conditions to expect. Use this information to plan your trip.

As you study your maps, determine where to obtain services—food, water, gas, ice, etc. Anticipate when you'll need to replenish fuel and supplies, and purchase them whenever you have the chance, since gas stations and stores are few in the vicinity of Mojave National Preserve.

Before you depart on a desert journey, leave a detailed itinerary with a friend or family member. Be sure to indicate when you expect to return; call later if your plans change.

WHEN YOU'RE THERE

Pay attention to your physical responses in the desert. Temperature extremes and dryness make it a stressful environment. If you're overweight or out-of-shape, take it easy, and don't push yourself to keep up with your fitter friends.

Although it's quite tempting, don't overschedule. There are so many places to explore in Mojave National Preserve. You could spend a lifetime and never see all of the sights in this 1.6-million acre spread. Planning a weekend whirlwind trip is likely to leave you feeling frustrated and exhausted. Pick one or two areas to explore during each trip, and plan to return again.

Hiking during the warmer months is best done in the early morning or late afternoon hours. During the heat of the day, try to find a place in some shade, and catch up on your reading, write in your journal, take a nap or enjoy a conversation with friends. It's not the time to be out on a strenuous hike.

WATER

Water is the essential life-sustaining substance in the desert. It's in short supply in this arid environment, and most natural water sources are probably unsafe to drink. Therefore, it's imperative that desert travelers be prepared at all times with sufficient quantities of water. An absolute minimum to carry is one gallon per person per day. Remember that a gallon of water weighs about eight pounds.

Anytime you venture out into the desert on foot, for even a short period, bring a bottle of water. Plastic bottles sold in backpacking and outdoors shops are convenient and easy to carry. It's far better to carry water and not need it, than to be stuck in an isolated area without a canteen. Bring enough water for each member in your party.

The key to staying properly hydrated outdoors is to drink before you become thirsty; take a few sips every 10 to 15 minutes or so. Don't ration your water, and don't waste it. Fill up when you have the opportunity (at campgrounds and at roadside rest stops; purchase water at stores when you can); it's a good idea to have more than you think you'll need.

FOOD

When packing food for desert travel, consider the dry climate, heat and cold you'll encounter. Additionally, consider nutritional requirements, tastes and appetite. Leave the junk, the sugary "treats" and empty calories at home. Better yet, leave them in the store, and choose instead healthy, high-quality fuel foods that are simple to pack and transport and easy to prepare.

You needn't go the dehydrated food route unless you're planning a backpacking trip where weight is a major concern.

DESERT SURVIVAL 97
Protein foods use more water for digestion than do carbohydrates; avoid meat, cheese, and peanut butter. Use dates, raisins, fruit or honey.

Pack plenty of trail mix, dried and fresh fruit, cut-up vegetables, whole-grain crackers and low-sugar cookies for trail snacks and light lunches. Cereal straight from the box, peanut butter sandwiches and other simple foods are camp staples. Boxes of juice pack and travel well. Remember that foods—especially bread, bagels and rolls—dry out quickly in the arid desert environment. Always wrap foods well before storing them.

If you bring a cooler and a stove, your food options increase dramatically. And if you are fortunate enough to have a willing camp cook in your party, you may be treated to the indescribable treat of scrambled eggs, hot coffee or chili prepared outdoors. Tantalizing as the thought may be, remember that you must use a stove or campground fire pits and grills. Bring your own fuel, charcoal or wood; do not gather wood in the desert.

Always pack and carry some food with you when you venture out into the desert.

CLOTHING

Heat, cold, wind and rain, cactus and rugged terrain characteristic of the desert combine to make proper dressing essential for protection and comfort.

Pack simple, sturdy clothing that doesn't show the dirt. Natural fabrics, especially cotton and wool, are favorite choices because of their breathability and durability.

The simplest approach to desert dressing

FLASHLIGHT

Depending on your habits, pack anything from a mini penlight to a large model complete with emergency flasher. Camp or candle lanterns are helpful, especially during the winter when days are short and nights are (very) long. Bring extra batteries, bulb and candles.

COMPASS

The indispensable tool for geographical orientation. If you know how to use it, bring a compass. If you don't know how to use one, learn how; outdoors shops and many organizations frequently offer map and compass classes. Increasingly outdoors adventurers are taking along various GPS (Global Positioning System) devices to help them stay oriented.

is to layer your clothing, adding to or subtracting from the layers as the temperature and wind allow. Make sure you choose roomy, comfortable clothing that doesn't bind anywhere. Classic long-sleeved button-front shirts and sweaters, T-shirts and tank tops are all smart choices, as are jeans and khakis. In general, long pants are preferred in the desert for the protection they offer from cactus and the sun, but long socks and hiking shorts may be more comfortable. Sweats are comfortable and warm in the early morning and evening hours.

What you wear on your extremities is as important as your body wear. In warm weather, head protection is a must. Popular choices include baseball caps, broad-brimmed canvas or straw hats. In cold weather, however, a knitted watch cap is best for keeping in your body heat; mittens or gloves make winter desert trekking more pleasant.

Selecting the proper footwear is always a question for outdoor adventurers. Desert hiking requires more substantial footwear than a pair of lightweight running shoes. The terrain is rough, and the temperature of the sand can really heat up during the day, making even short hikes literally a blistering experience. Sturdy hiking boots or the hiking shoes manufactured by running-shoe companies are good choices. Since waterproof materials are rarely required for desert hiking, the fabric-and-leather construction of these running shoe-hiking boot hybrids is ideal. These lightweight boots breathe, and can be much more comfortable than heavy-duty waffle stompers. Look for long-wearing soles and stiff shanks for comfort and support.

Pack running shoes or other comfortable footwear to wear around camp.

Above all, when selecting footwear, get a proper fit. Improperly fitting boots or shoes will never be comfortable. Period.

Outerwear is largely a matter of personal choice. Modern synthetics and polar fleece have been fashioned into jackets, pullovers and pants. They offer maximum protection from the elements, with minimal weight or bulk. Down jackets and vests are also popular and comfortable for cool weather or nighttime desert wear. Windbreakers offer inexpensive protection from the almost ever-present winds in the Mojave Desert; they are easily stuffed into a day pack or fanny pack.

Many desert rats swear that their most valuable piece of clothing is a bandanna. These brightly colored squares of cloth can serve as a handkerchief, neckerchief, towel, washcloth, headband, loincloth, bikini top, sweatband, head scarf, tablecloth, napkin—well, the list is limited only by your imagination . . .

DESERT HIKING

The very notion of walking the desert in general, and Mojave National Preserve in particular, is a surprising one to some

MAPS Because Mojave National Preserve covers such a vast territory, a good map is indispensable. The Auto Club's San Bernardino County map is useful for getting to the preserve, as well as around it to the major sites. Tom Harrison's Recreation Map of the Mojave National Preserve and the Trails Illustrated/National Geographic map of the preserve are two excellent detailed maps that every visitor will find useful.

The USGS topographic maps cover most of the area, but since the preserve sprawls over more than a dozen maps, they tend to be inconvenient. Also, the new preserve and wilderness boundaries are not on these maps.

The BLM offers a series of California desert maps/guides. They're particularly useful for desert destinations outside the preserve boundaries.

PHONE As of 1999, your basic cell phone could call out from about one-third of Mojave National Preserve. Remember, Mojave is a desert of mountains, so don't expect miraculous coverage.

SUNGLASSES

They protect from the intense light, glare, and wind so characteristic of Mojave. Polarized lenses and UV ratings between 50 and 80 ensure real protection, not just stylish looks. Attach a leash to your glasses for convenience.

people—even to some avid hikers. The desert that seems so huge from a car, can seem intimidating on foot.

Apparently not that intimidating though; reader response to John McKinney's *Los Angeles Times* hiking columns about the preserve proved to be enthusiastic to say the least! More walks "way out there" readers demanded.

With such a desert, the visitor really needs two views: the broad view offered by an auto tour, the intimate view offered by a sojourn afoot.

Throughout this guide, we've suggested some favorite walks: to Amboy Crater off old Route 66; along willow-lined Aiken Wash; to—and into—the unusual Lava Tube; around the grounds of the old Zzyzx resort; along the Mojave River near Camp Cady and many more.

These walks are leg-stretchers, informal wanderings, part of the grand tour. We hope that you heed some of our suggestions, get out of car and walk as much as possible.

The preserve also offers some longer, half-day and all-day walks. Some of these walks are suitable for the whole family, others are for experienced hikers in good condition.

Although the preserve has only two signed hiking trails (Mid-Hills to Hole-in-the-Wall and Teutonia Peak), roads (closed to vehicles), washes, and narrow canyons are excellent footpath subsitutes.

For the very experienced desert hiker,

- **Emergency Supplies** Extra food and water, which you may wish to keep in your vehicle all the time. Waterproof matches, fire-starting tablets, a well-stocked first-aid kit and a couple of blankets.
- **Toilet paper** and tissues
- **Sunscreen** Get the SPF rating that's right for you, and use it. Reapply frequently.
- **Lip balm** To protect from chapped lips, look for one containing a sunscreen for best protection.
- **Skin lotion** To counteract the drying effects of the desert.
- **Camera** Always bring more film than you think you'll need, along with an extra battery.
- **Insect repellant** Keeps the critters off you.
- **Sewing kit** Buttons pop off when you least expect it.
- **Notebook or journal and pen** A good place to scribble your thoughts and take notes about your observations in Mojave National Preserve.
- **Daypack or fanny pack** Easy to carry on a day hike; keep an extra water bottle in each for convenience.
- **Binoculars** for bird-watching
- **Telescope** for sky-watching
- **Any prescribed medications**
- **And always, a good book.** As you read through this guide, you'll notice quotes from some favorite desert classics.

there are some excellent Class 2 and Class 3 climbs and cross-country routes. Providence and New York peaks are two fine climbs; these peak-bagging expeditions are for experienced hikers in top form with route-finding abilities. By all means, if you are one of these experienced hikers, get yourself some topo maps and an ample water supply and go for it!)

For the average day hiker, there's a week or two's worth of wonderful walking in and around the preserve. From the cool, mysterious environs of Mitchell Caverns to the magnificent Joshua Tree forest and the boulder-strewn Caruthers Canyon, the pre-

POCKETKNIFE

What comes in handy more frequently than a trusty Swiss Army knife? Enough said.

Not even the early AAA touring bureau drivers, responsible for mapping and assisting fellow travelers, were exempt from getting stuck in the sand.

serve offers the hiker a surprising diversity of terrain.

This desert has a way of making every trip an adventure. If you like the idea of walking to places where it seems there's no one else for miles around, or where you could swear no one has ever been before, Mojave National Preserve may be just the place for your next hike.

DESERT DRIVING

Because there are so few amenities available in and around the preserve, you must not only bring your own supplies, but consider your automobile a self-contained "survival module." Be certain that your vehicle is road-worthy and capable of withstanding harsh desert conditions. In case of emergency, your life could literally depend on it.

The image of bouncing across the desert in a dilapidated old jalopy may have some romantic appeal; it symbolizes the highly cherished notion of the freedom of the open road. In reality, however, driving a well-maintained, comfortable and reliable vehicle provides a sense of confidence and security—and a real measure of safety as well.

Naturalist Joseph Wood Krutch described venturing into the desert as "rewarding travel in an unfrequented land." Travel in the desert is rewarding for a number of reasons, not the least of which is the fact that it truly is an "unfrequented land." The wide-open spaces and lonely desert roads are particularly appealing to those seeking the solitude and quiet the desert offers.

But in an unexpected situation, such as a vehicle breakdown, that feeling of peaceful solitude can quickly become a fearful experience in a hostile environment. Therefore, driving a road-worthy vehicle is of utmost importance in the desert.

Mojave National Preserve is bounded by two major highways. Since the area is fairly isolated from cities, it's probable that any vehicle that's driven the one hundred-plus miles it takes to get there is in pretty good shape. But venturing into the desert, far from highway services, requires some special preparation.

The perils of desert driving include extreme heat and glare (especially when driving east in the morning or west in the afternoon); winter cold, ice and snow. The

Know your limits – and those of your vehicle – and don't push them, or this could happen to you.

long, straight roads can become monotonous and sleep-inducing day or night. Dirt roads require special driving skills, and the unfamiliar territory demands navigational expertise. Weather conditions, including dust, wind and thunderstorms which can cause flash floods, are other difficulties faced by desert drivers.

A HISTORICAL PERSPECTIVE

In the early days of automobile travel in the desert, none of the roads were paved. Little more than trails—sometimes marked with signposts—the roads gave drivers a real adventurous ride through the desert. The earliest autos weren't even equipped with tops or windshields, and electric lighting systems did not come into use until 1912. Still, intrepid individuals made their way to the Mojave for spirited travel experience.

A 1911 Stanley Steamer – durable enough for desert travel, even when loaded with family and friends.

Over the years, travelers have been advised to carry equipment and supplies to cope with emergencies. Earliest autos were notoriously unreliable; a 1914-1917 Auto Club checklist suggested carrying two stout pieces of rope, each 10 feet long, a collapsible bucket for radiator water, and two wide canvas strips, each about 100 feet long sewn together (for getting unstuck).

In the 1946 book *A Guidebook to Route 66* by Jack Rittenhouse, the author offered "a few small tips which mean big comforts: DON'T WORRY! A trip is no fun if worry sits at the wheel, even if this worry is not voiced to others in the car. So first of all rest assured that you're not going to be 'hung up' in some forsaken spot. You'll never be more than a score of miles from gas, even in the most desolate areas. There are no impossible grades."

MAP READING

A U.S. Geological Survey report circa 1900 noted, "With some persons, the faculty of getting lost amounts to genius. They are able to accomplish it wherever they are. The only suitable advice for them is to keep out of the desert. There are safer places in which to exercise their talent." If those words strike home, remember that map-reading is a skill. And like any other skill, performance improves with practice.

Certainly there is nothing more nerve-wracking or upsetting than the experience of a frustrated driver demanding directions

EQUIPMENT CHECKLIST

Although today's better maintained, more reliable vehicles may not be as prone to breakdown as those in the past, many of the precautions suggested over the years still apply today. An up-to-date checklist includes the following:

- a well-maintained vehicle
- recent oil change
- recent tune-up
- good battery
- check all fluid levels: water, coolant, oil, etc.
- check all belts; carry a spare fan belt
- check tires, carry a good spare, jack and tools
- check suspension
- check windshield wiper blades
- carry repair manual, extra water and coolant for the vehicle; if you carry extra gasoline make sure it's in a proper container
- carry flares, fuses, blankets, extra food and water, tools and an up-to-date Automobile Club or emergency services membership

from an unsure navigator. Not only is it frustrating, but potentially hazardous, especially when intensified by traffic, hot weather, fatigue or confusing territory.

To avoid such disorienting and upsetting scenarios, spend time before departure planning and mapping out excursions. Write down directions, road names and numbers and pertinent landmarks to prevent on-the-road confusion. While the main access roads to Mojave are well-marked, many lesser roads are not signed at all. Therefore, pay close attention to mileage on the odometer when following directions to locations throughout the desert.

ROAD CONDITIONS IN MOJAVE NATIONAL PRESERVE

The main roads in Mojave (Essex, Kelbaker and Kelso-Cima) are paved. Many other main roads (Ivanpah and Cedar Canyon, for example) are not. They are graded, and usually easily passable by the typical sedan. Other lesser roads in the desert are gravel, unmaintained dirt that can become very soft and rutted, or passable by four-wheel drive only. Therefore, the driver's experience and the type of vehicle must be considered carefully when mapping a route and choosing roads.

Keep in mind, as you drive through the desert, to take it easy. Don't try to drive too far, too fast or too long. If you get tired, pull over and rest or switch drivers for awhile. If you become disoriented, stop, regroup, consult the maps and examine landmarks to become re-oriented once again.

In 1937, photographer Edward Weston traveled extensively throughout the West. His wife, Charis, kept a journal, and her observations make it clear that while vehicles have improved immeasurably, driving in the desert hasn't really changed much. "Luckily traffic was not heavy—each of the two cars we did meet left powdery dust sifting down on us for ten minutes after."

Outdoor lovers agree that it's impossible to know the land unless you venture off the highway and explore it. Nowhere is that more true than in Mojave National Preserve. Only after you leave the main roads that bound the "lonesome triangle" can the appeal of the place become clear. It seems to speak to the all-American pioneer spirit that lives on to this day.

Interstate 15

I-15 is the northern boundary of Mojave National Preserve. The primarily 70-mph speed limit highway is the major route taken between Barstow and the state line by Las Vegas-bound travelers from Southern California. It's also a stretch of highway that provides access to a number of unexpectedly pleasant desert destinations.

BARSTOW

I-15 anchors the westernmost point of Mojave National Preserve at Barstow, population 20,000, where fast-food stands, restaurants and motels line Main Street. It's a major supply point, a place to purchase food, gas, film and provisions before you head into the desert for an extended stay.

During the 1950s, America launched its Interstate Highway system. These gals and CHP officers are celebrating the opening of I-15.

Barstow Station on the east side of town is the locale of a gargantuan McDonald's serving up Big Macs in converted railroad cars. The station also has a tourist information outpost. Once a small-time railroad town, Barstow is fast developing into a major desert city. Preserve visitors can avail themselves of the supplies and amenities available from what is by far Mojave's largest "gateway town." For more Barstow information, call (888) 4-Barstow (422-7786).

Barstow's new status as a gateway town to Mojave National Preserve accounts for only a fraction of the city's recent and rapid growth; instead, economic stimulus comes from the presence of the U.S. Army Training Center, Marine Corps Logistics Base, NASA's Goldstone Deep Space Network, the Burlington Northern-Santa Fe Railroad Yards and 120 factory outlet stores.

In their desire to lure would-be guests and gamblers from metropolitan Los

Silver
Dry
Lake

Baker

SODA MTNS

Soda
Dry
Lake

Soda
Springs

Zzyzx

Rainbow Basin
National
Natural Landmark

Afton
Canyon

Mojave

River

Calico
Ghost Town

Calico Early Man
Archaeological Site

CADY MTNS

Yermo

Barstow

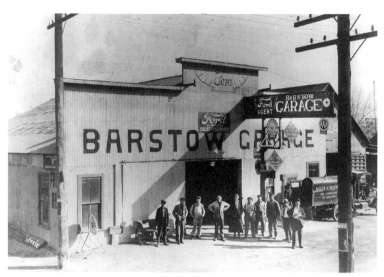

1912 view of the Barstow garage. Today the city is the major gateway to Mojave National Preserve.

Angeles to Las Vegas as quickly as possible, some Nevada casinos publish highway maps that depict both Baker and Barstow as little dots in the desert.

This biased cartography often leads the motorist who's new to the eastern Mojave to two mistaken conclusions: (1) There's nothing but a wasteland along I-15 between San Bernardino and the Nevada state line, and (2) Barstow and Baker are the same puny size.

Actually, Barstow dwarfs Baker with its much greater population, and number of services, restaurants and accommodations. Barstow boasts more than 30 restaurants, plus a dozen fast-food outlets.

Barstow has about 20 motels, many of them offering rather low-cost accommodation, as well as several nearby camping opportunities

CALIFORNIA WELCOME CENTER AND DESERT INFORMATION CENTER

The California Welcome Center is a logical first stop on a west-east desert tour. Maps, informative brochures, information about the preserve and other nearby desert areas, camping, lodging and desert attractions, along with a selection of guidebooks are available.

The welcome center is located off I-15, just south of downtown in the midst of a major mall—the Tanger Outlet Center.

CALIFORNIA WELCOME CENTER
2796 Tanger Way
Suite 100
Barstow, CA 92311
(760) 253-4813

MOJAVE RIVER VALLEY MUSEUM

Founded by local citizens in 1964, this eclectic museum is dedicated to preserving and interpreting the heritage of the Mojave River Valley. Exhibits include archeological artifacts from the nearby Calico Early Man Site; locally found gemstones and minerals, including agates, jaspers and turquoise; and photographs of city pioneers. A collection of publications and local crafts are available for purchase at the museum.

MOJAVE RIVER VALLEY MUSEUM
Corner of Barstow Road and Virginia Way, Barstow
(760) 256-5452
Hours: 11-4 daily; closed Tuesday and Wednesday

RAINBOW BASIN

The designation on the map of "National Natural Landmark" is a tip-off, but nothing can prepare you for the sight of the spectacular series of colorful hills that comprise Rainbow Basin. Pink, white, orange, brown red, black and green sediments form the basin's rainbow-colored walls. The subtle colorations, the greens and browns, are due to the differing oxidation rates of iron.

These towering hills, exquisitely formed and appearing to be hand-painted, are seen from the signed three-mile, one-way loop drive. You could spend a pleasant weekend camping and hiking in Rainbow Basin. Stationed at Owl Canyon Campground is a campground host who can provide hiking and touring tips. This superb place in the Calico Mountains is ideal for the hiker to sample the mountains, spectacular geology and rich historic record of the eastern Mojave Desert.

Some 15 million years ago, grasslands filled Rainbow Basin, which was populated by saber-toothed tigers, mastodons, camels, three-toed horses and even rhinoceros. Their fossil remains are encased in sedimentary rock that once formed a lakebed. As a result of intense geologic activity over the millenia, what was once at the bottom of the lake is now a series of folded, faulted, colorful hills.

Colorful Owl Canyon – great for a short stroll or a full weekend of camping and hiking.

Owl Canyon (five miles round trip to Velvet Peak with 500-foot elevation gain) is one of three moderate hikes in Rainbow Basin. This canyon takes its name from the barn owls who live there. Hikers should be reasonably agile in order to tackle Owl Canyon Trail, because getting through the canyon means scrambling over some boulders.

To visit Rainbow Basin, follow Interstate 15 to Barstow, then join Highway 58 to Fort Irwin Road, following it five miles. Turn west on dirt Fossil Road and proceed

The folded and faulted landscape of Rainbow Basin invites exploration. Closer examination reveals the fossil remains of many animals embedded in the rocks.

three miles to Owl Canyon Campground. The trail begins at the north end of the campground.

Follow the marked trail into Owl Canyon. Half a mile up-canyon look for a small cave on your right.

Sandstone and siltstone, shale and volcanic debris are among the exposed rock visible to the hiker. The geologic formations en route are not only rainbow-colored but dramatic in shape. Particularly evident are massive downfolds geologists call synclines.

The canyon narrows for a time then opens up at its end into a multi-colored amphitheater. Velvet Peak is the high spot above the rocky bowl. Experienced hikers can scramble up the bowl's rocky ridges for fine views of Rainbow Basin and the vast Mojave.

RAINBOW BASIN NATIONAL NATURAL LANDMARK

10 miles north of Barstow. (From Highway 58 in Barstow, take Fort Irwin Road north 5.5 miles to Fossil Bed Road. Follow signs approximately 3 miles to the Landmark; take 3-mile-long scenic drive.)

CALICO GHOST TOWN

7.5 miles east of Barstow (Exit I-15 at the Ghost Town Road exit; follow signs 3 miles north to the park.) Fees for parking and admission.
P.O. Box 638
Yermo, CA 92398
(760) 254-2122
Hours: 9-5 daily

The stone tools of Pinto man found on the shores of Lake Manix.

CALICO GHOST TOWN

Calico, a one-time boomtown that produced more than $86 million from its silver mines, went bust just after the turn of the century. The town has been restored, and today it's a regional park operated by San Bernardino County.

The town features several western-style shops, restaurants and attractions, including a mine tour, playhouse, railroad and museum. Some of the original 19th-century buildings are still standing: the saloon, town office, country store and general store.

Calico hosts a number of regularly scheduled events, including a Hullabaloo (the weekend before Easter), the Spring Music Festival (Mother's Day weekend) and Calico Days (Columbus Day weekend).

This Wild West tourist stop attracts vistors from all over the world. On any given day, you may overhear French, German, Japanese or Italian.

CALICO EARLY MAN SITE

Prehistoric stone tools found at the Calico Early Man Archeological Site—scrapers, hand picks, choppers and the like—have been estimated by a tiny minority of scientists to be up to 200,000 years old. The site's authenticity is highly controversial among anthropologists and archeologists, who heatedly debate the topic of Early Arrivals vs. Late Arrivals. Nearly all present-day scientists fall into the "Late Arrivals" camp and estimate that humans arrived in

Tour leader explains how Dr. Louis S.B. Leakey ordered archeological work to be conducted, one square foot at a time. This digging site is 25 feet deep.

this part of the Mojave Desert no more than 10,000 to 12,000 years ago.

Nevertheless, Calico was the only place in North America where the famed archeologist/paleontologist Dr. Louis S.B. Leakey chose to work. Known primarily for his work in Olduvai Gorge in East Africa, Leakey directed the excavation of the site from 1963 until his death in 1972. The National Geographic Society funded the project.

A visit to this site is an introduction to the tedious, methodical work of archeologists, a process unknown to many of us. Working with hand tools no bigger than toothbrushes and awls, archeologists have recovered some 11,400 artifacts, moved uncounted tons of earth, kept meticulous records, and dug some 26 feet into the earth—three inches at a time.

A tour of the site is guaranteed to raise incomprehensible questions about the origins of human life and the passage of an unfathomably long period of time. It's an experience that is simultaneously enlightening and disturbing, inspiring and quite profound.

CALICO EARLY MAN ARCHEOLOGICAL SITE

15 miles northeast of Barstow via I-15 (from the Minneola Road exit, follow the signs north 2½ miles along graded dirt roads to the site). Hours: open for guided tours Wednesday 1:30 and 3:30pm; Thursday-Sunday 9:30 and 11:30am and 1:30 and 3:30pm; closed Monday and Tuesday
For group tours, write to: Friends of Calico Early Man Site, P.O. Box 535, Yermo, CA 92398.

LAKE DOLORES WATERPARK

(take the Harvard Road exit) 72 Hacienda Road, Newberry Springs, CA 92365; (760) 257-1233

Afton: the "Grand Canyon" of the Mojave.

LAKE DOLORES WATERPARK

Here's a place to cool off. Boasting the world's largest raft ride, as well as a dozen more rides and slides, the waterpark is I-15's newest attraction. Those who just can't wait to get across the state to the Colorado River, can tube down the waterpark's Lazy River or pedal a paddle boat across Lake Dolores. The park has a couple of food outlets and is constructing an RV campground.

AFTON CANYON

Afton Canyon, located near the western boundary of the preserve, is a pleasant place for a day hike or an extended stay (for greater detail, see Mojave River Basin chapter).

The canyon, under the stewardship of the U.S. Bureau of Land Management, features a steep-walled gorge cut by the once-

mighty Mojave River, and is often referred to as "the Grand Canyon of the Mojave." The river runs here year-round, allowing cottonwoods and other riparian vegetation to flourish.

SODA SPRINGS/ ZZYZX

Formerly a cavalry outpost and later a health resort run by radio minister Dr. Curtis Springer, Soda Springs today is a part of the preserve that's administered by the California Desert Studies Center, a field station of the California State University. The self-contained, energy-efficient facilities include classrooms, science labs, a complete kitchen and dormitory space.

Originally conceived as a research facility for use by university faculty and students, the center has evolved into an educational retreat for those interested in all facets of desert study. The center is under the administration of the Department of Biological Science, CSU Fullerton.

Occasionally, ranger-led weekend tours of the Soda Springs facilities are offered. Tours include information about the area's natural history, human habitation, plants and animals, as well as insights into the colorful history of the former resort.

BAKER

A small desert town, Baker is a good point to fill up your gas tank, purchase supplies, and make last-minute preparations before entering Mojave National Preserve.

AFTON CANYON
33 miles east of Baker (Take the Afton turnoff from I-15, then the 3-mile dirt and gravel road that's washboard in places; parking in the BLM's Afton Campground)

SODA SPRINGS/ ZZYZX CALIFORNIA DESERT STUDIES CENTER
60 miles northeast of Barstow (exit I-15 south on unpaved, graded road for 4 miles to the center)

This colorful sign once pointed the way to Dr. Springer's place. Today's I-15 travelers are intrigued by the less provocative Caltrans Zzyzx sign.

Accommodations and food are available in Baker; for a tasty surprise, stop at the Mad Greek restaurant. Order a Greek salad, a souvlaki or zucchini sticks and marvel at your good fortune; imagine finding such tasty food and pleasant surroundings in what many would consider the middle of nowhere. The other landmark is the long-established Bun Boy restaurant.

Across the street looms the world's tallest thermometer: 134 feet high, not coincidentally reaching 134 degrees, the highest reported temperature in the northern hemisphere recorded nearby in Death Valley.

Located right near the giant thermometer is the Mojave National Preserve Desert Information Center. Here you'll find maps and information about the preserve and other desert public lands, along with a

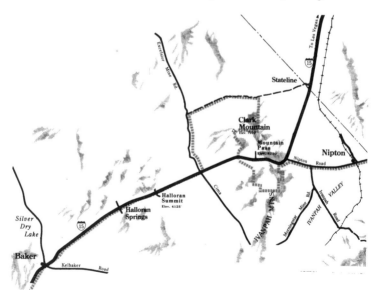

national park ranger to answer your questions and a Death Valley Natural History Association bookstore.

Baker is a good departure point for desert exploration. Highway 127 heads north toward Death Valley National Park. Many visitors choose to begin their Mojave National Preserve adventure by taking Kelbaker Road, which heads southeast of I-15 out of Baker and leads straight to Kelso Depot (34.5 miles), and Kelso Dunes (44.7 miles) in the preserve.

Halloran Springs, an extremely small settlement just off I-15, between Baker and Cima Road, offers gas and water.

At the Cima Road exit is a small settlement known as Valley Wells; facilities include food, water, gas, a small store and a phone.

MOJAVE DESERT INFORMATION CENTER
72157 Baker Blvd.
P.O. Box 241)
Baker, CA 92309
(760) 733-4040

NIPTON

Located just two miles from the California/Nevada border, Nipton is the kind of desert settlement that often appears on television or newspapers as a human interest spot. The town's motto is "Where the past is present." It's perfectly appropriate, especially when the midnight freight train rumbles through.

Nipton was founded in 1904 with the coming of the San Pedro, Los Angeles and Salt Lake Railroad. A small community sprang up at the Nipton railhead to serve the local mining, ranching and railroad workers.

From hard rock miner to "mayor" of Nipton: Jerry Freeman welcomes guests to the town he purchased in 1984.

NIPTON

(exit I-15 at Nipton Road; 10 miles to the town) Contact Nipton Station, Route #1, P.O. Box 357, Nipton, CA 92364; (760) 856-2335

These days Nipton is growing under the leadership of geologist Jerry Freeman who purchased the town in 1984 and restored the hamlet's hotel and store. Ask for an interpretive pamphlet at the store, and take a stroll through Nipton history past the old buildings.

Hotel Nipton, where silent film star Clara Bow was a frequent guest, is a pleasant Southwestern-style bed-and-breakfast. For a hedonistic desert treat, the hotel even offers an outdoor hot tub.

Nipton also boasts a small campground that includes four overnight hook-ups for RVs plus several more sites with fire rings and picnic tables. Nippeno Camp, as its known, can also accommodate overnight guests in a couple of "eco-shelters"— platform cabin tents.

Nipton: A place for rest, relaxation, and reflecting on the beauty of the desert.

Purchase provisions and catch up on all the local news at the Nipton Trading Post. The creation of Mojave National Preserve has put little Nipton back on the map, and the town is evolving into a kind of gateway community for Mojave visitors.

PRIMM

Beyond the turnoff to Nipton, I-15 bends north and heads for Vegas. But before Glitter City, the highway takes you to what was once aptly named Stateline on the California-Nevada border, and now known as Primm. Here you'll find—"can't miss" would perhaps be a better way to put it—Whiskey Pete's, a casino–hotel–restaurant–truckstop in ersatz Wild West decor, and boasting of "Nevada's loosest slots." Primm Valley Resort and a huge outlet mall for discount shopping also vie for your attention, along with a monorail and a roller-coaster.

For what it offers guests, Primm has costly accommodations; I-15 travelers will find better and far less expensive lodging in Barstow, Baker, and even Las Vegas.

CAMPGROUNDS OFF I-15

Barstow/Calico KOA Campground
7 miles northeast of Barstow via I-15 and Ghost Town Road
(760) 254-2311
72 tent and RV spaces

Calico Ghost Town Regional Park
1.5 miles southwest of Calico off I-15
(760) 254-2122
200 tent and RV spaces

Afton Canyon
35 miles northeast of Barstow off I-15 on Dunn Road
(760) 256-3591
22 tent and RV spaces

Owl Canyon
10 miles north of Barstow via Highway 58 and Irwin Road
(just south of Rainbow Basin)
(760) 256-3591
31 tent and RV spaces

Caltrans Rest Areas on Interstate 15:
• Approximately 30 miles northeast of Barstow
(just west of Afton Canyon)
• Approximately 20 miles northeast of Baker (just west of Cima Road)

7

Interstate 40

While Interstate 15 offers any number of interesting sites and tourist attractions, Interstate 40 provides a different type of route. This nearly straight shot from Barstow to Needles leads through a desolate land of mountain ranges and big sky country that is often crisscrossed with vapor trails from the military jets that frequently swoop through the area.

I-40 is the southern access route to Mojave National Preserve. Three roads—Kelbaker, Essex and Goffs—lead north into the desert.

Heading southeast down I-40 from Barstow, you'll soon drive through the United States Marine Corps Logisitics Base, then on past the futuristic Solar One facility,

Until a gas station and store recently opened in Fenner, this sign was true.

Southern California Edison's solar power plant. The Fort Cady Road exit, about 35 miles from Barstow, is the last place for gas, lodging and food until Ludlow, 27 miles to the east. At Ludlow, gas, lodging and food are available; until recently, when a gas station/food store opened in Fenner, it was the last service stop on I-40 until Needles, 100 miles away! Be very sure to check your water supply, along with gas and oil levels, before heading east.

Twenty-seven miles east of Ludlow, the Amboy-Kelso exit leads to Kelbaker Road. Kelbaker Road climbs through Granite Pass (elevation 4,024 feet), and down toward Kelso (elevation 2,126 feet) and the heart of the preserve. Kelbaker, the preserve's major north-south thoroughfare, extends all the way from I-40 to I-15 at Baker.

Forty-eight miles east of Ludlow, Essex Road is the entry point to Providence Mountains State Recreation Area and Mitchell Caverns.

Essex Road is a convenient entrance point for traveling to the popular campgrounds at Hole-in-the-Wall and Mid Hills, easily reached from Black Canyon Road, just off Essex Road.

The quirky movie "Bagdad Cafe" was filmed at the Sidewinder, where you can still get home cooking. Before the 1987 release of the movie, the former town of Bagdad had one claim to fame: the longest recorded period of not even a drop of precipitation in 767 days (1909 to 1912).

GOFFS ROAD AND GOFFS

Fifty-five miles east of Ludlow, Goffs Road leads to the small town of Goffs, and on to Lanfair/Ivanpah Road which leads toward the heart of Mojave's onetime min-

Fenner, an oasis of sorts on a lonely stretch of I-40.

Historic Goffs Schoolhouse – newly restored.

ing district. Goffs Road also provides the most direct access to Fort Piute to the east.

Fenner is the hamlet located at the Goffs Road exit off I-40. A gas station and market with a fish pond out back welcome travelers from all over the world. Step inside the market to find Naja's Food and Drink, a small eatery that prepares veggie burgers and (compared to just about anything else along the interstates) fresh and healthy sandwiches.

Goffs, once a steam locomotive watering stop, is now home to fewer than two dozen people. At the Goffs General Store and Country Kitchen, limited supplies—including ice and short-order meals—can be purchased. The store, with its pot-bellied stove and friendly atmosphere, is a social center of sorts for this end of the preserve.

Robert Ervin, a retired construction expert for the Los Angeles Housing Department, renovated the Goffs Store and

reopened it in 1998. "I wanted to move out of Los Angeles to a peaceful place like Goffs," Ervin explains. "There's no hurry-up here."

In *The Thousand-Mile Summer*, Colin Fletcher wrote: "In the last rays of the setting sun, the cluster of buildings that was Goffs did not look the sort of place to be unduly worried by automobiles. Or for that matter, to be worried by anything much."

Be sure to visit the tan-colored Goffs Schoolhouse, a one-room desert schoolhouse constructed in 1914. The school, in operation for 23 years, also served as a community center and even as a branch of the county library. Over the years the school building fell into serious disrepair. Thanks to the efforts of the Mojave Desert Heritage and Cultural Association, the schoolhouse was meticulously restored in 1998. Adjacent to the schoolhouse is a

Goffs General Store revitalized by new owner Robert Ervin (top).

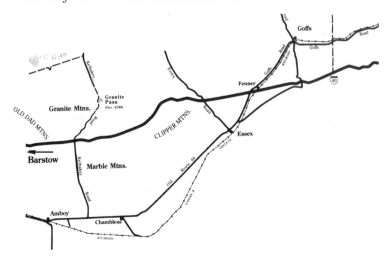

windmill and an eclectic collection of Mojave Desert ranch implements, Route 66 paraphernalia and a plaque proclaiming Goffs "the Desert Tortoise Capital of the Mojave Desert."

The schoolhouse restoration and Goffs' ongoing historical interpretation efforts have been, and are, spearheaded by historian and Goffs resident Dennis Casebier. Casebier's five-decade long collection efforts of Mojave Desert historical material has resulted in an invaluable library of some 6,000 books, 20,000 historical photos, as well as hundreds of recorded oral histories, periodicals and newspapers.

NEEDLES

The aptly named Needles – distinctive spiked mountains east of town.

Named for the spikey mountains to the east of town, Needles is situated just west of

the Colorado River. Historically, by virtue of becoming an early railroad town and transportation center, Needles (more so than Baker and Barstow) was the early and long-time "gateway" to the eastern Mojave, and to the land we now call Mojave National Preserve.

For more than a century, Needles has been a railroad town and transportation center.

Needles was established in 1883 when two railroad companies constructed tracks to the Colorado River; the Atlantic & Pacific laid tracks from the east, the Southern Pacific from the west. A few years later, the A&P, and a portion of the Southern Pacific, were acquired by the Santa Fe Railroad. According to the most recent City of Needles economic profile, the Santa Fe Railroad, after more than a century, remains the area's largest employer.

Needles occasionally makes the national news when it records the nation's hottest temperature. Daily maximum temperatures average more than 100 degrees F. in June, July, August and September.

Many find these warm temperatures to their liking—particularly retirees who settle here as well as snowbirds from Canada and other cold climes who flock to the Needles area to spend the winter months.

Needle's traffic count is high as a result of its geographic positioning between the mushrooming boomtown of Laughlin Nevada to the north, and popular Lake Havasu with its London Bridge to the south. The city, in close proximity to Colorado River watersports, offers all auto-

MOJAVE NATIONAL PRESERVE, NEEDLES INFORMATION CENTER
707 W. Broadway
Needles, CA 92363
(760) 326-6322

CAMPGROUNDS OFF I- 40

Desert Drifter RV Park
Take Daggett exit off I-40; 34805 Yermo-Daggett Rd., Daggett, CA 92327;
(760) 254-3200
80 tent and RV spaces

The Dellwood Travelers Motel & Campground
Take Fort Cady exit, then .25 mi. west on National Trails (old Rt. 66) 47800 National Trails, Newberry Springs, CA 92365
(760) 257-3348
18 tent and RV spaces

Needles KOA
1.5 miles northwest of Needles on National Trails Highway
(760) 326-4207
88 tent and RV spaces

Park Moabi
Park Moabi Road
Needles, CA 92363
(760) 326-3831

motive services as well as plentiful and inexpensive lodging.

Mojave National Preserve maintains an administrative office and visitor information center in downtown Needles. Located on W. Broadway along an intriguing stretch of old Route 66, the center offers information, publications, and the latest weather and road conditions.

U.S. HIGHWAY 95

This north–south route, to the east of the desert, is the main road to Searchlight (Nev.) and on to Las Vegas. (Beware there is also an Arizona 95; this sometimes confuses travelers) There are services in the town of Cal-Nev-Ari. A point of interest along the route is at Ibis, site of the desert military war game maneuvers led by General George S. Patton in 1942. A historic marker commemorates the site about five miles north of I-40.

One interesting "backdoor" route into Mojave National Preserve is Highway 164 which leads west into California and the tiny town of Nipton. The highway climbs over the McCullough Range and descends to an impressive Joshua-tree-dotted high plain.

8

Route 66

No other road in all of America has inspired more dreams than Route 66. The 2,200-mile asphalt ribbon once stretched from Chicago to Los Angeles and set free the imagination of dreamers all over the nation. It opened up the modern-way west to California.

The Route 66 trip takes longer than the I-40 route. But, because it offers a unique view of days gone by, take the time. Pull over, get out of the car, sit by the side of the road, and listen to the quiet. It's an eardrum-pounding quiet that cannot usually be perceived. Take in the sight of the barren land, the many mountain ranges, the alien volcanic territory near Amboy Crater. Allow yourself to feel the eternal, un-

changed quality of this land. This desolate stretch of highway gives no hint of the metropolis just 200 miles to the west, but it's easy to imagine both the fears and the hopes of the countless travelers who once journeyed across this road, dreaming of a better life.

Most of those who journeyed west on Route 66, Dust Bowl migrants, first-generation children of immigrant parents, wanderers, drifters and vacationers, were a bit frightened by the prospect of crossing the Mojave Desert. In the 1946 volume, *A Guide Book to Highway 66* by Jack D. Rittenhouse, the author observed, "You won't find any desert stretches which are blistered with unendurable heat. Worst stretch is the Mojave Desert, 200 miles of territory running west from the California-Arizona line. . . . To many easterners, the desert is a terrifying thing, but to many who frequent the region the desert is a thing of majestic beauty." In *The Grapes of Wrath,* John Steinbeck wrote, "And 66 goes on over the

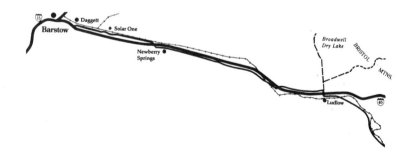

terrible desert, where the distance shimmers and the black cinder mountains hang unbearably in the distance."

Long-shuttered cafés dot the length of old Route 66.

The stretch of Route 66 from just outside Barstow to just west of Needles is the longest stretch of the historic route in California. "How far between towns?" wrote Steinbeck, "It is a terror between towns." It's hardly a terror today, and it's well worth getting off the high-speed interstate to drive through what used to be known as "America's Main Street."

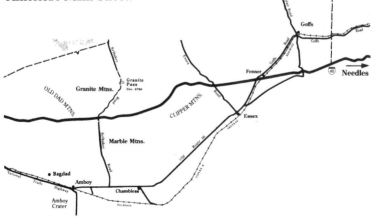

Telephone lines, poles topped with glass insulators, parallel the highway, a reminder of why the route was once termed "the Wire Road." Mountain ranges appear far in the distance; abandoned gas stations, diners and motels dot the route. The tiny settlements that sprang up along this route did so primarily to serve the needs of the travelers that came through. Rittenhouse wrote, "Except for Ludlow, no 'towns' worthy of the name existed between Needles and Daggett, California, a stretch of 150 miles."

Route 66 is still within sight of the interstate from Newberry Springs to Ludlow, but as you travel east through Ludlow, Amboy, Cadiz, Danby, Essex and Fenner—all just off the highway—the trip down Route 66 becomes a journey into America's past.

Ludlow is a good supply point, as described earlier in this guide. About 28 miles east of Ludlow, you'll notice extensive Hawaiian-like lava fields. Amboy Crater, the cause of this flow, lies just south of the road.

AMBOY CRATER

We're fascinated by volcanoes and, as long as they're not too hot and not active, we like to visit them. Amboy Crater, located out with the old-time diners and abandoned gas stations along historic old Route 66, has long been a curiosity for generations of desert travelers.

The little volcano can be reached with a short hike (three miles round trip with

200-foot elevation gain), an ideal leg-stretcher for motorists desiring a break from interminable Interstate 40.

Many of the black cinder mountains (and red ones, too) are now part of the Mojave National Preserve, though Amboy Crater is outside the preserve and under the jurisdiction of the U.S. Bureau of Land Management's Needles office.

On the drive to Kelso and into the heart of the preserve, the volcanically inclined visitor can count a dozen or two cones and a number of lava flows.

Amboy Crater and environs are covered with two kinds of lava: *aa* (pronounced *ah-ah*), sharp, hiking boot assaulting hunks of basalt and *pahoehoe* (pa-hoy-hoy), smoother, rope-like lava.

While it's difficult to get lost because Route 66 and Amboy Crater are almost always in view, it is possible to get quite frustrated if you get sidetracked in the lava field labyrinth and end up involuntarily extending your short hike to the volcano. It's only a little more than a mile from the parking area to the crater, but it can seem much longer if you do a lot of zigzagging over the lava. Forget trying to follow any one path and instead make a bee-line for the base of the crater. Look back occasionally to establish landmarks to assist you on your return trip.

To reach Amboy Crater from Barstow, head east on Interstate 40 some 52 miles and take the Ludlow exit. Join National

Trails Highway (the modern moniker for old Route 66) and drive 28 miles southeast to just short of Amboy and the intersection with Amboy Road. Turn south on a signed dirt road leading 0.4 mile down a short graded road. Proceed slowly this road (littered with sharp, potentially tire-shredding lava chunks)to a dirt parking area.

From the parking area, follow the vehicle road, which soon ends in a spaghetti-tangle of trails. Eyeball the crater and simply start walking straight toward it. The hiker will soon figure out that the easiest traveling is over the smooth sandy stretches between the rough lava flows.

Approaching the cinder cone, angle right toward Amboy's west ridge. A footpath climbs to a wide opening in the crater rim. Climb into this breach in the cone, then continue on this west side to the rim. Walk along the rim for panoramic vistas of the surrounding lavascape and the eastern Mojave Desert. Continue walking clockwise around the rim, then retrace your steps back to the parking area.

AMBOY AND ONWARD

The town of Amboy, about five miles east of the crater, has never consisted of much more than a café or two and a motel. A huge sign announces "Roy's Motel and Cafe." Built in the mid-'40s, the stop has always been a popular one with tourists. Gas is still available here. About 2.5 miles east of town, Kelbaker Road extends south to Route 66; take it for access to Kelso and the Mojave National Preserve.

Between Amboy and Essex, you'll notice abandoned autos, closed-down diners and service stations. The buildings may still stand, but the spirit and life behind them appears to have just dried up and blown away-exactly what happened when 66 was bypassed by the interstate.

Essex, about 25 miles east of Amboy, has a cafe, a small store and a post office. Essex Road leads to the Providence Mountains and Mitchell Caverns.

Route 66 continues another 13 miles past Essex to Mountain Springs Summit where it rejoins I-40.

9

Getting Oriented to the Preserve

A majority of the preserve's highlights are accessible by paved roads or well-maintained dirt ones. A visitor could easily spend a day, a weekend or a week exploring the preserve's scenic splendor without needing a four-wheel drive vehicle.

Five main paved roads cross Mojave National Preserve: Kelbaker, Cima, Ivanpah, Essex and Goffs (half-dirt). For the most part, these roads lead visitors in a north-south exploration of the preserve. Four roads converge at Kelso, future site of the Mojave Visitor Center.

Kelbaker Road, between I-40 and I-15, receives the heaviest use. On weekends, motorists use the road to "cut through" the preserve en route to and from Las Vegas and Palm Springs.

The preserve's paved roads, along with 80 miles of dirt roads, are maintained in good condition by San Bernardino County. The National Park Service maintains another 20 miles or so of connector roads leading to such major visitor attractions as Kelso Dunes and Zzyzx.

In 1989, when the U.S. Bureau of Land Management administered the Mojave, Wildhorse Canyon Road, which loops from Hole-in-the-Wall Campground to Mid Hills Campground was declared the nation's first official "Back Country Byway."

Soon after Wild Horse Canyon Byway was designated, seven more Back Country Byways were added to the then-East Mojave National Scenic Area: Kelbaker Road, Kelso-Cima Road, Black Canyon Road, Cima Road, Ivanpah-Lanfair Road, Essex Road, and Cedar Canyon Road.

By the early 1990s, Mojave's eight-byway system soon totaled a somewhat astonishing 222 miles—the most extensive system in the West. While the National Park Service does not designate its scenic roads as "Backcountry Byways," the beauty of these roads remain, and offer preserve visitors some truly grand motor tours. These roads crisscross the desert and lead to, or close to, most of Mojave's major scenic attractions. The preserve's major and minor roads are covered in detail in the touring chapters of this guide.

Prior to the establishment of Mojave National Preserve in 1994, a road inventory counted some 2,180 miles of paved and dirt road within the preserve boundaries. After the preserve was formed, approximately 345 miles of dirt road traversing newly declared wilderness areas were closed to vehicle entry. Some of these dirt roads are becoming part of the preserve's wilderness footpath system.

MOJAVE ROAD

Challenging the four-wheel drive enthusiast is the Mojave Road, a 140-mile-long route that visits many of the most scenic areas in the preserve. The rough dirt road was reconstructed and is now maintained by the Friends of the Mojave Road.

The road uses the historic trade route followed by Native Americans as they

The Mojave Road attracts desert drivers who love Mojave's wide-open spaces.

crossed the desert on their way to the coast. Spanish and Western explorers, miners and mail carriers used the route; eventually settlements and military outposts were established along the road. Today, the Mojave Road stretches from the Fort Mojave Indian Reservation on the Colorado River, west to the former military outpost at Camp Cady.

Along the way, it passes through or near some of Mojave's most memorable places, including Fort Piute, Mid Hills, Cinder Cones, Soda Dry Lake and Afton Canyon.

Traveling along the Mojave Road provides access to remote areas of Mojave, and an experience of the land that is not possible to gain if the visitor only stays on major roads.

The route is marked with cairns (piles of rocks), but your best guide is the *Mojave Road Guide,* written by Dennis Casebier and the Friends of the Mojave Road.

The Mojave Road is a rugged route through desert wilderness. Driving on it requires planning, desert driving experience and appropriately equipped vehicles. It should never be attempted without a group of fellow travelers. Mountain bikers have ridden parts of the Road, and hikers have walked on it, but the Mojave Road is primarily a route to be explored in a four-wheel drive vehicle.

WILDERNESS

When Congress passed the California Desert Protection Act in 1994 and established Mojave National Preserve, nearly half the preserve—some 700,000 acres—was set aside as wilderness. By legal (and somewhat lyrical) definition:

"A wilderness, in contrast with those areas where man and his works dominate the landscape, is hereby recognized as an area where the earth and its community of life are untrammeled by man, where man himself is a visitor who does not remain."

In the case of Mojave National Preserve, wilderness entry and use restrictions are similar to those in some of the nation's other wilderness areas. Some provisions allow Native Americans the use of motor vehicles to gain access to sacred sites located in wilderness areas; private property holders in certain instances may traverse wilderness to reach their property.

Mojave's wilderness offers outstanding opportunities for hiking, scientific study, education and recreation. Wilderness roads closed to mechanized vehicles are now pathways to adventure for those willing to explore this wondrous land one step at a time.

CAMPGROUNDS

Hole-in-the-Wall and Mid Hills are the preserve's two developed campgrounds and a fee is charged for their use. Both camps have been recently, and significantly, up-graded by the National Park Service.

Hole-in-the-Wall's 35 campsites can accommodate large recreational vehicles and are accessible to campers with disabilities. A RV dump station, new restrooms and a greatly improved water system, add to the camper's convenience. Equestrians enjoy a group campsite with a corral.

Mid Hills Campground and its 26 sites is oriented to tent campers and visitors with small RVs. It, too, has much-improved restrooms and water system.

ROADSIDE CAMPSITES

Hundreds of traditionally-used back-country roadside campsites are scattered throughout the preserve. Preserve policy allows such roadside camping at any "previously disturbed" campsites. Absolutely no improvements (trash containers, picnic tables, restrooms, etc.) have been made to these campsites.

Picking sites that have already been used for camping helps protect the desert from further damage. Please don't camp along paved roads, or in day-use areas, and respect the rights of private property owners.

FIVE FAVORITE ROADSIDE CAMPING AREAS

Rainy Day Mine Site (3 to 4 sites) Head 15.2 miles south of Baker on Kelbaker Road. Turn north on the road leading to Rainy Day Mine (4x4 vehicles only) and travel 0.3 mile.

Black Canyon Road (3 to 4 sites) 5.2 miles south of Hole-in-the-Wall Ranger Station on the east side of Black Canyon Road.

Granite Pass From I-40, travel 6.1 miles north on Kelbaker Road. Just north of Granite Pass, you'll find access roads on the west side of Kelbaker Road. Campsites are located just north of the granite spires.

Caruthers Canyon (4 to 6 sites) Head 5.5 miles west of Ivanpah Road on New York Mountains Road, then 1.5 to 2.7 miles north of New York Mountains Road to campsites. RVs not recommended.

Sunrise Rock From I-15, head 10.4 miles south on Cima Road. Campsites are locates on the east side of the road nearly opposite the trailhead for the Teutonia Peak Trail.

Ranger Sean McGuinness

TIPS FOR VISITORS

by Mojave National Preserve
Chief Ranger Sean McGuinness

Mojave is a great place for an escape. The mountains and vast valleys, cinder cones and sand dunes offer opportunities for hiking, climbing, camping, four-wheeling, nature study and much more.

Use this guide to become familiar with this vast preserve and to seek out a special spot away from it all that uplifts your spirit.

Park rangers are present to help visitors appreciate the natural and cultural wonders of Mojave, as well as to enforce park rules. They are dedicated to ensuring that your park experience is both safe and enjoyable.

Familiarize yourself with the rules and regulations that protect you, your fellow visitors, and the fragile desert environment:

• Mojave is a National Park Service unit that is protected by the same federal regulations that apply to all of America's national parks. All plants, animals, rocks, historical objects, buildings, archeological artifacts, and other natural and cultural objects are protected by law. Please leave all such objects and living things intact, and do not disturb them in any way.

• Vehicles, including motorcycles and bicycles, are permitted on open roads only. Please respect all wilderness boundary markers while driving. All motorized vehicles must be "street legal" and have valid license plates and highway registration.

• Roadside Camping is allowed. Select

sites that have been traditionally used for camping, not along paved roads or in day-use areas, and stay at least one-quarter mile from all water sources.

• Wood is scarce in the desert; the collecting or cutting of wood is not permitted. Bring your own firewood to the preserve. Campfires are allowed in fire rings in developed campgrounds and at other established sites. Backpackers and roadside campers are encouraged to use camp stoves rather than build fires for cooking.

• Pets must be leashed at all times.

• Hunting is allowed in Mojave National Preserve. The discharge of weapons is allowed only while legally hunting. No "plinking" or target shooting is permitted. The California Department of Fish and Game regulates hunting throughout the state of California; please refer to the agency's current regulations. A current California state hunting license is required. Be prepared to present your hunting license and tags to federal or state officials if requested to do so.

• About 45 percent of the preserve is federally designated wilderness. Exploration by foot or on horse is encouraged to experience the solitude and scenic beauty of these special places. Cars, bicycles, and other mechanized vehicles are not allowed. Wheelchairs can be used in wilderness areas.

Part III

On Tour

10

Mojave River Basin

The Mojave River was formed thousands of years ago when the climate of the area was considerably wetter than it is today. When the San Gabriel and San Bernardino Mountains were being formed, the increased rainfall enhanced the size and power of the river. The river deposited alluvial materials, wore down mountains, and cut gorges along its path. Afton Canyon, a beautiful, 600-foot deep canyon, was carved through the surrounding hills of solid granite. It's an impressive example of the power of the once-mighty Mojave.

The river emptied into the ancient Lake Manix, then meandered eastward into Lake Mojave (seen today as Soda and Silver dry

Mojave River during wetter times and climes was a river of considerable size. Even in today's arid climate, the Mojave manages to flow above ground in a few places, including Afton Canyon.

lakes), and finally joined with the Amargosa River in Death Valley, both of which emptied into another ancient lake, Lake Manly. Changing weather patterns at the end of the Pleistocene, a few million years ago, caused the lakes to dry up, and the river to become a relative trickle compared to its former size.

The banks of Lake Manix, along with the alluvial and bajada formations created by the flowing water, can be viewed from the northern edge of the eastern Mojave (outside the preserve) between Calico and Baker. One excellent vantage point is the Calico Early Man Archeological Site, where artifacts and the story of ancient dwellers make the land come alive.

Some 15,000 to 75,000 years ago during a hot and much more humid climate,

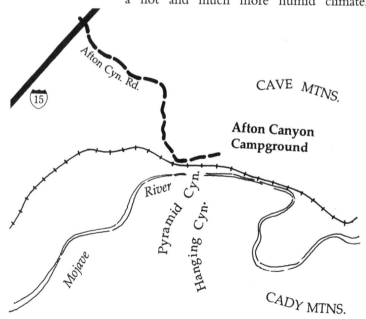

wildlife was abundant around the lake, which was shallow, but about 200 square miles in size. Turtles, shellfish, camels and antelope flourished. It's almost surreal to imagine a flock of pink flamingos, all standing on one leg, looking over a landscape that Great Inagua of the Bahamas than the Great American Desert.

Archeological evidence uncovered along the former banks of the river and ancient lakebeds indicates that not only did it support a large population of indigenous people, but it served as a trade route between present-day Arizona and the coast. The Mohave people left enormous piles of mussel shells, which they gathered on the shores of the lake. They also cultivated crops at the mouth of the Mojave River.

The Mohaves regularly came into contact with people who followed the river west. Cultural artifacts including pot shards, arrow points, choppers and scrapers, which were created by Mojave River people, have been found alongside ceramics, turquoise, bows and arrows fashioned by the Anasazi to the east. Further evidence of Anasazi influence has been disovered at the turquoise mining site at Turquoise Mountain, north of Halloran Springs.

As the climate became more arid, the Mohave were forced to move toward the Colorado River to continue their way of life.

Today, the river is much less mighty than it once was. From the river's headwaters in the San Bernardino National Forest, at the Mojave River Forks Recreation Park and Flood Control Dam, the Mojave flows some 150 miles eastward, only a fraction of which is above ground. Just east of Afton Canyon, the river ends at Soda Lake in Mojave National Preserve.

AFTON CANYON

Afton Canyon Natural Area, 42,000 acres under the administration of the U.S. Bureau of Land Management, borders Mojave National Preserve on the northwest, and is one of the most conveniently located sites in the eastern Mojave. Don't miss stopping here! (Afton Canyon and Mitchell Caverns in Providence Mountains State Park are the two most intriguing environments bordering Mojave National Preserve and a visit to one/both is very much a part of the preserve experience.)

Take the Afton exit off Interstate 15, 33 miles east of Barstow; the graded three-mile-long road leads to the campground in Afton Canyon. Park at the campground, being careful not to take a campsite.

The narrow, corridor-like Afton Canyon has been referred to as the "Grand Canyon of the Mojave." It is an eight-mile-long, narrow gorge with sheer walls that rise 600 feet above the canyon floor. When he passed through the canyon in 1776, Fr. Garcés wrote, "I went five leagues in a west-southwest direction and came to pass through the mountains. Streaks of different-colored minerals can be seen on the mountainside. I named it 'Sierra Pinta.'"

Fr. Garcés, diarist for the De Anza Expedition that explored California and founded Mission San Gabriel, was not the only historic figure to travel through Afton Canyon on his way from the Colorado River to the coast. A half-century later, Jedediah Smith followed the Mojave and after getting a bit exasperated with the river's habit of disappearing underground for long stretches, called it, most aptly, "The Inconstant River." Kit Carson took the river route, as did John C. Frémont, who gave the Mojave its name.

William Adams Vale, who kept a journal during his trip through the desert, noted, "I walked down the canyon looking at caves and deep gorges in the mountains. . . . Oh! What a country—there is some grand scenery in Cave Canyon."

Afton Canyon is one of the few places where the Mojave River runs year-round. The lush growth found here prompted Fr. Garcés to write, "Here grows the wild grape; where there is much grass, also mesquite and trees. . . ."

The dependable source of water supports a variety of plants including cottonwoods, willows, rabbit bush, smoke trees and grasses. For more than a decade, botanists and hard-working volunteers have waged war against the invasive tamarisk which threatens to choke out native species. The labor-intensive program, which

The best views of Afton Canyon are obtained by train (above) or on foot (below).

requires cutting the tamarisk with a chain saw and the immediate application of an herbicide, will eventually result in a more oasis-like streamside community.

The plants that grow in the canyon provide shelter for many species of wildlife. Migratory birds are attracted to the site, as are several other species of birds, including stream-frequenting herons, egrets, killdeer and ibis. California mud turtles, frogs, minnows and the Mohave chub live in the river or along the shore, and bighorn sheep travel down from the mountains to water in the area. The shy bighorn have been frightened off by the motorcycles that once took over this campground, and now career over adjacent Rasor OHV Area.

The Mojave Road in Afton Canyon has been re-routed in order to protect the sensitive riparian environment, and off-highway vehicles have been prohibited in the area due to significant damage that has been caused by irresponsible riders in such places as "Competition Hill," which can be seen on the approach to the canyon.

Railroad aficionados will delight in the number of freight trains that regularly pass through on the tracks that run the length of the canyon. The sight and sound of a mighty locomotive powering across gleaming trestles are practically unforgettable.

Afton Canyon features a number of smaller, side canyons formed from water draining out of the nearby Cady Mountains. It's been said that it would take a lifetime to find and explore all the little side canyons adjacent to Afton Canyon.

There are two main hikes in Afton Canyon Natural Area: the hike up Pyramid Canyon (3.5 miles round trip), the major side canyon, and the hike through large Afton Canyon (6.5 miles round trip or longer and shorter jaunts). You may also explore the side canyons to the north and south of Afton Canyon.

Pyramid Canyon, the deepest and largest of the side canyons, can easily be located and hiked. Cross the river under the first set of railroad trestles, just south of the campground. The scenic water-eroded formations of this canyon make it especially enjoyable. Raptors, including golden eagles and red-tailed hawks, can often be seen circling in this area. And rockhounds have long considered the canyon a rich site for gathering specimens, among them agates, geodes and Mexican sapphires.

Although there's no real trail up Pyramid Canyon, simply follow it to its rocky end, a bit less than two miles from Afton Canyon. Improvise your route; the canyon is so wide that you may walk up one side and return to the trailhead on the opposite side.

The water-cut, eight-mile length of Afton Canyon is an intriguing out-and-back hike; if you follow it to its end, it's a 16-mile round trip full-day hike, but most hikers prefer sampling the canyon with a more modest 5- to 6-mile jaunt. The short

Pyramid, one of Afton's scenic side canyons.

walk along the riverbed from the campground to the railroad trestle is a favorite exploration suitable for the whole family.

As you hike the canyon, you'll view an old mine on the south wall of Afton Canyon. Although it appears to be an abandoned gold mine, the owner of the mine simply salted it with gold in order to sell worthless shares to unwitting investors.

Continuing east, you'll notice a number of side canyons situated on the north wall of Afton Canyon. These side canyons are most obvious when you look for the man-made culverts that have been placed to prevent further water erosion. At the culvert marked 192.99, is another canyon that features magnificently eroded shapes caused by thousands of years of wind and water. At the culvert marked 194.65, take a flashlight to explore a fascinating cave/canyon that twists and turns; just when you think it ends, it turns once again and keeps going.

Beyond this point the canyon widens and holds less interest for the hiker. Afton Canyon extends a few more miles to a double trestle bridge near Cave Mountain. For a different perspective of the canyon, consider returning via the river bottom.

CAMP CADY

Located off the I-15 Harvard Road exit, the Camp Cady area takes in part of the Mojave River floodplain where desert willow, cottonwoods and tamarisk flourish. Today, the land is owned and maintained by

the California State Department of Fish and Game. The agency has plans to develop nature trails here, but at present, hiking and bird-watching opportunities require a bit of improvisation.

Since this photo was taken, Camp Cady has deteriorated markedly.

Camp Cady was once the westernmost of the string of tiny military forts established during the 1860s to protect westbound settlers and travelers. The post has been reduced to a crumbled corner of rocks chinked with mud nestled in a stand of willow trees.

This boat was left high and dry when the Mojave River receded.

Turn-of-the-century Greek immigrant, movie theater magnate Alexander Pantages (of the famed Hollywood Pantages Theatre) built a thoroughbred horse ranch and an enormous stable at this site. You can just imagine the sight of the pampered animals being put through their paces in this out-of-the way place.

Theater magnate Alexander Pantages raised thoroughbreds at his ranch. The California Department of Fish & Game now maintains a field station here.

Owls have taken up residence in this water tower.

A hike through this river floodplain reveals evidence that people lived throughout this area not so long ago: A ramshackle lean-to here, a thatched willow hut there, rusted-out abandoned vehicles and even a boat or two. Yes, boats; the Mojave River not so long ago had enough water to permit rowboats and motorboats to patrol this territory that in places resembles the setting for the classic movie *The African Queen*.

The resident bird population, along with the seasonal migratory short-term residents makes this a prime area for birdwatching. You may spot hawks, quail, owls and several other species; the endangered Mohave tui chub inhabits the ponds, as do frogs and mud turtles.

The Fish and Game staffers headquartered here are responsible for this 2,000-acre site, and for studying the bighorn sheep population in nearby mountains.

11

Soda Springs/Zzyzx

Because of its year-round supply of fresh water, Soda Springs has long been a stopping point for west-bound travelers, settlers and desert dwellers. It's a preserve highlight.

Soda Dry Lake is the largest playa in Mojave. The term 'dry lake,' however, is a misnomer; the lake's surface is often muddy and wet. It is located just east of the Mojave River Sink, where the Mojave begins to flow underground.

Among the flattest landforms in the world, playa lakes are created under ultra-arid conditions when water suddenly drains into basins (having no outlet) and rapidly evaporates. Soda Lake begins where the Mojave River ends.

During wet years, the visitor will observe standing water atop the playa. In drier times water, which lies very near the surface of the playa, is drawn upward by that phenomena we vaguely remember from middle school science texts—capillary action. The playa's water often rapidly evaporates, leaving behind a white puffy crust of sodium bicarbonate. This shimmering white surface often adds a mirage-like appearance to Soda Dry Lake.

Located six miles southwest of Baker, about 60 miles northeast of Barstow, Soda Springs has a long and colorful history. Native people have lived here for thousands of years; their tools, cairns and cleared areas, known as "sleeping circles," date back to the Pleistocene Period, 8,000 B.C. Their descendants left archeological evidence of

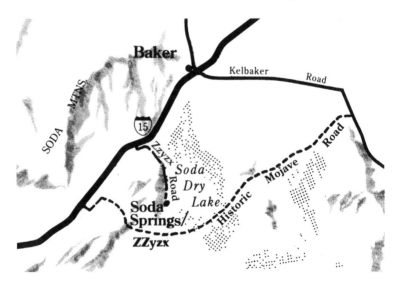

continued occupation through the mid-1800s.

As was the case throughout the West, when settlers, trappers and explorers traveled through, clashes occurred with native peoples who were tied to their ancestral homelands. In 1860, the U.S. Army established an outpost at Soda Springs known as "Hancock's Redoubt." Intended to escort travelers along the Mojave Road, as well as U.S. Mail carriers, the outpost was described as "a series of breastworks and corrals constructed of mud and willow-brush." Decommissioned after 1868, the outpost became a commercial rest stop-known variously as "Soda Station" and "Shenandoah Camp"—for travelers.

The Tonopah and Tidewater Railroad, which ran north from Ludlow to Silver Lake, was built by Francis "Borax" Smith in 1905. The railroad was created to transport iron ore and passengers; to serve the needs of travelers, a station was built in Soda Springs. It lasted less than a year, and closed in 1908. The railroad, however, continued to run until the early 1940s, when the tracks were torn up and used as scrap metal during World War II.

Dr. Springer broadcasted his folksy philosophy on his radio show originating from Zzyzx.

ZZYZX MINERAL SPRINGS & HEALTH RESORT

Soda Springs then entered a colorful new era that was to last some 30 years, from 1944 through 1974. Thanks to the efforts of the white-suit-wearing Dr. Curtis Springer, Soda Springs became much more than an

Springer claimed the fish in his lake were "health-conscious." He advised guests to bait their hooks with sun-dried raisins rather than salmon eggs.

Dr. Springer marketed his Antediluvian herb tea as an integral part of his seven-day cleansing plan. He reminded the faithful, "Health is wealth."

ANTEDILUVIAN TEA

The Body Beautiful

oasis. It was turned into a resort that promised health to its thousands of visitors and financial supporters. Known as Zzyzx Mineral Springs and Health Resort, Springer's development in the middle of the desert was established on the basis of mining claims registered with the government.

Springer may have gotten the idea for the health resort and mining claim from reading comments of travelers through Soda Springs. Lt. Robert Williamson wrote in 1853 of "several fine springs, slightly brackish but not unpalatable." The next year, Lt. Amiel Weeks Whipple wrote, "the dry bed of the lake is covered with efflorescent salts, probably sulphate of soda." But he wasn't the first to come up with the notion of using the water at Soda Springs for therapeutic purposes. In 1871, an article about Soda Springs appeared in the San Bernardino Guardian. "The boys have built for the use of the public a nice bathing place and invited us to take a bath while they are preparing dinner."

When Springer and his wife, Helen, arrived at Soda Springs in 1944, they described it as a "mosquito swamp." A few old buildings remained from previous ventures in the area, but the couple began to develop the place into a self-contained town unlike anything else in the Mojave.

A labor force recruited from L.A.'s Skid Row—each man was paid $10 per week—built the resort's extensive facilities. A 60-room hotel called The Castle, a dining hall, indoor baths and a large swimming pool shaped in the form of a cross were among the original projects. Springer broadcast his daily religious programs from his powerful radio station, and conducted services at the Zzyzx Community Church. Since there were no utility services, the entire development was self-contained and energy-efficient.

The main road in the complex was named "Boulevard of Dreams," and for many years it was a fitting title. For thirty years, believers, health-seekers and the curious flocked to Zzyzx, lured by Springer's promises and products. "Our Hot Mineral Water baths, matchless climate and wonderful foods await you and remember a condition that has been coming on for years cannot be corrected in days so plan on staying with us long enough to give our facilities a chance to help," read a 1961 Springer brochure.

Wearing his trademark white suit, Springer always greeted his guests with a smile and a wave.

Although the self-proclaimed "old-time medicine man" never attached a fee to his concoctions or services, the donations poured in; "Freely you have received, as God makes possible, Freely Give," read the sign on a coin box placed on an exit table. It's been estimated that Springer's annual income ranged from $250,000 to $750,000.

Eventually, the powers-that-be began questioning Springer's methods and claims. "Doc Springer," as he was known to his detractors, was charged with income-tax evasion by the Internal Revenue Service; he was called "King of the Quacks" by the American Medical Association; he was convicted of false advertising by the Pure Food and Drug Administration; and his claim to the land and his Zzyzx facilities were finally confiscated by the Bureau of Land Management.

Despite a long, bitter court battle, including a lengthy article penned by Springer entitled "The Legal Rape of Zzyzx," he never returned to the resort after he was evicted in 1974; he died in 1985.

SODA SPRINGS TODAY

The Desert Studies Center is a field station of the California State University system and operated as a cooperative venture with the National Park Service. Established in 1976, the center is managed by the California Desert Studies Consortium, an organization of seven Southern California CSU campuses: Dominguez Hills, Fullerton, Long Beach, Los Angeles, Northridge, Pomona and San Bernardino.

The Desert Studies Center can accommodate a maximum of 75 people. Some of Springer's buildings are still in use, although many have been rebuilt or improved; a new shower and kitchen have made the facility more comfortable for visitors.

Most overnight visitors are students enrolled in university-level, desert-related science classes or researchers exploring desert topics. Sometimes school groups or community groups with a desert mission or cause can be accommodated at the center.

Wildlife biologists find the Soda Springs area of great scientific interest. The minnow-sized Mojave Tui chub survives in shallow ponds along with another Mojave native, the Saratoga Spring pupfish. Desert Studies Center birdwatchers have recorded sightings of more than two hundred species in Mojave National Preserve.

Soda Springs and vicinity is habitat for a high number of reptiles, including five lizards—zebratail, whiptail, leopard, chuckwalla and collared, as well as five snakes-shovelnose, sidewinder, speckled rattlesnake, gopher and red racer.

Soda Springs offers a wide diversity of nearby environments to study: creosote

The rooms that once housed health seekers and sun worshipers now serve as dormitories for student researchers and scientists.

Field research is often grueling work, but the rewards may be a new clue to the life of early man.

scrub, ponds and springs, sand dunes, mesquite thickets. The rocky slopes and ravines of the Soda Mountains offer two more intriguing environmental niches to explore.

The subjects of the Center's scientific inquiries are as diverse as the desert's environments. Scientists tackle pre-Cambrian fossils, Cima's volcanic origins, as well as studies of the behaviors of desert ants, kangaroo rats, dragon flies, the spotted toad and many more creatures.

Weekend tours of Soda Springs/Zzyzx are sometimes conducted; contact a Mojave National Preserve Visitor Information Center for details.

12

Kelso and the Heart of the Preserve

Situated in the heart of Mojave National Preserve are two scenic wonders: Kelso Depot and Kelso Dunes. One man-made, one natural, both stand as reminders of the inevitability of change over time. Easily accessible from good roads, they are the most frequently visited sites in the preserve.

If Mojave National Preserve had a Main Street, Kelbaker Road would be it. The road is the preserve's busiest, and provides access to several of the most popular attractions. In early 1999, the National Park Service installed a large Mojave National Preserve entry sign just outside of Baker on Kelbaker Road. The entry monument, one of those grand granite proclamations characteristic of other western national parks, emphasizes Kelbaker's status as the major Mojave road.

Most preserve visitors remain in their vehicles while driving Kelbaker Road from Baker to Kelso Depot and thus miss a couple of interesting sights en route. Two of our favorite sights along the way are the Kelbaker Hills and the Lava Beds.

"KELBAKER" HILLS

Here's your chance to name one of the preserve's geographic features. We call them the Kelbaker Hills because of their proximity to Kelbaker Road, as well as for their

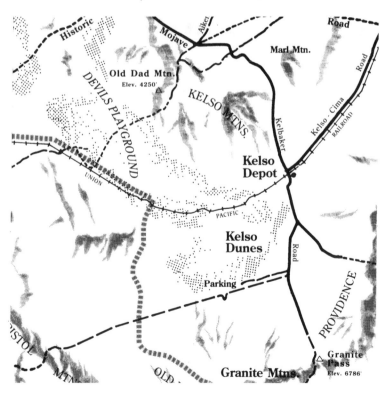

location a dozen miles southeast of Baker and two dozen miles northwest of Kelso; however, they don't really have a name on the map or one in common usage. Others have suggested the "Baker Hills" due to their close-to-town position or the "Rhyolite Hills" because of their volcanic composition.

Out-of-the-way sights in out-of-the-way places. A jack-o'-lantern greets a hiker in the Kelbaker Hills.

By whatever name, these hills offer a close-to-the-paved road wilderness experience, as well as a short (2 miles round trip with a 300-foot elevation gain), though moderately strenuous, hike.

To access the Kelbaker Hills from Baker and I-15, drive 11 miles east on Kelbaker Road. Just as the road makes a pronounced bend right (south) turn left (north) on the unsigned dirt road. Drive 0.8 mile along the preserve's signed wilderness boundary. Look east of the road for a distinct gap in the Kelbaker Hills and scarce parking just east off the road where you can find it.

If you locate a sketchy old road extending east up the wash leading to the hills, take it; otherwise, simply walk up the wash toward the obvious gap in the hills. Your route will angle toward the base of the tallest hills, and just to the left of them.

A bit more than 0.5 mile out, you'll observe a couple of narrow ravines (favorite burro routes, judging by the tracks) that lead to the top of the hills. Climb (careful, it's loose footing) any one of these ravines for good views of this part of the preserve.

Experienced rock-scramblers can make their way to the top of the highest hills. Those determined to make a loop hike out of this jaunt can do so by descending a ravine southeasterly, joining the main wash that leads back to the gap in the hills, and then returning to the trailhead.

LAVA BEDS

Another Kelbaker roadside attraction is the preserve's northern lava beds. A wash extending alongside the lava formation provides the hiker with a close-up view of the volcanic cliff face, as well as a convenient thoroughfare for the short (1.2 miles round trip with 100-foot elevation gain) hike.

This look at the lava resembles those hillside cuts made by highway-makers, though it was nature, not a road crew, that revealed the lava beds. Green, gray and red lichen color the north side of the lava outcroppings.

From Baker and I-15, head 14.2 miles south on Kelbaker Road to the Lava Beds and an unsigned turnout on your left. The turnout is just south of the long, narrow beds and just north of a wash. (Hint: if Kelbaker Road takes you through a major gap in the Lava Beds, you ventured about 0.4 mile too far south of the trailhead for this little exploration.)

Head east on a faint, but visible trail at the base of the lava beds. Marvel at the odd geology as you walk 0.6 mile to trail's end.

Scramble to the top of the lava beds and

a miniature plateau paved with a mosaic of lava talus that resembles the ruins of an ancient Roman Empire road. Make your way west cross-country over the plateau. Just short of Kelbaker Road, descend from the plateau by scrambling down the rocks to the trailhead.

KELSO DEPOT

In 1906, the completion of the railroad between Salt Lake City and the port facilities in Los Angeles led to the modest development of the tiny town of Kelso located, as the railroad described it, "235 track miles from Los Angeles." As the only railway between the two major cities, it grew in importance with the emergence of Los Angeles as a major urban area. Because Kelso was one of the few places in the desert with access to dependable water sources, it was considered a good location for a railroad stopping point.

Kelso Station, located "235 track miles from Los Angeles," seemed a veritable oasis to passengers crossing the desert by train.

Steam locomotives, still in wide use at the time, took on boiler water in Kelso before they chugged up the long Cima grade-a climb of 2,000 feet in eighteen miles. Later, railroad officials realized Kelso was a good location for a stopover point for railroad crews to rest and obtain supplies.

Kelso became an important railroad stop for several reasons. In the early 20th century, before the debut of diesel-electric locomotives, huge, powerful steam locomotives (which required enormous and regular infusions of water for their big boilers) had

The one-room Kelso Schoolhouse also served as home for the teacher (circa 1908).

This baggage wagon helped move luggage and supplies at Kelso.

quite a struggle to get up steep hills and over mountain passes. Stiff grades, such as that up Cima Hill east of Kelso, required the addition of a helper locomotive to aid freight and passenger trains.

At Kelso, helper locomotives were coupled to the front of eastbound trains to assist in the climb to the summit of Cima, located 18 miles away, and 2,078 feet higher, than Kelso. After gaining the summit, the helper locomotives would be uncoupled, then turn around on rails north of the main line. The helper locomotives would then barrel westward light (without cars) back to Kelso Depot. Sometimes the helpers pulled into a round house, a kind of garage for locomotives, where mechanics performed maintenance and repairs.

Actually, Kelso's location was not perfect for railroad purposes; the more ideal locale is at the bottom of the grade at Cork, 28.7 miles west; however, Kelso had the only dependable water supply, fed by deep wells and a water table that extended from the Providence Mountains to the southeast.

The Spanish-style depot was built by the Los Angeles and Salt Lake Railroad (part of the Union Pacific system) in 1924. Originally known as the Kelso Club House and Restaurant, this distinctive 50-by-150-foot, two-story stuccoed structure was designed with a red-tiled roof, graceful arches, and a red brick platform. It featured several small rooms that provided overnight accommodations for railroad employees, a billiard room, library, a telegraph office, and a waiting room for passengers.

Nicknamed "The Beanery," the restaurant served meals to passengers traveling on trains without dining cars. Several large rooms located in the basement of the facility served as a community center for local residents.

Keeping the depot's restaurant supplied with foodstuffs was no easy task. The railroad itself transported dishes, silverware, linens, employee uniforms and Omaha beef from its commissary in Omaha. Fruits, vegetables, dairy products and other fresh foods were shipped to Kelso from Los Angeles.

During the war years, the population of Kelso increased to nearly 2,000 residents-primarily railroad employees and workers at the Vulcan Iron Ore Mine located in the nearby Providence Mountains. The railroad was used extensively to haul the mined ore to its milling site in Fontana. But when the mine shut down in 1947, the town's population dwindled. Rail services also declined.

The depot continued to be open through the mid-1980s, although it ceased to be a railroad stop for passengers after World War II. Visitors picnicked on the oasis-like lawn, ate at the restaurant and generally enjoyed the Mediterranean ambience of the charming building. When Union Pacific officials decided to demolish the historic structure in 1985, local citizens, governmental officials, environmentalists and a host of others formed a coalition to

fight the plan. The group, known as the Kelso Depot Fund, was successful in its efforts to save the depot. The U.S. Bureau of Land Management assumed ownership of the depot in 1992; it passed to the National Park Service in 1994 upon creation of Mojave National Preserve.

After extensive restoration, the old depot will be used as a visitor information center for Mojave National Preserve. A museum emphasizing railroad history and food service will adjoin the new visitor center.

Located at the intersection of Kelbaker Road and Kelso-Cima Road (Mojave's two primary trans-preserve roads), the new Kelso Depot visitor center is ideally located. While extensive restoration efforts are necessary to convert the depot, such efforts are well worthwhile because the architec-

Graceful Kelso Depot awaits restoration – and rededication as a visitor center.

tural integrity of the depot has remained intact.

The availability of water at Kelso makes it an important stop for migratory birds; the lawn and cottonwood trees provide an oasis-like feeling. And the historic architecture lends a stately elegance to the once-again tiny town with a population of only two dozen. Although they rarely stop here, freight trains regularly rumble through Kelso, adding a nostalgic touch to this picturesque setting.

KELSO DUNES

One of the most spectacular and popular sights in Mojave National Preserve is Kelso Dunes. This 45-square-mile formation of magnificently sculpted sand dunes is among the most extensive dune fields in the West. Some dunes tower over 700 feet high.

The dunes are actually built up from the particulate remains of mountains worn away long ago. Prevailing winds create the dunes as they blow sand particles from the Mojave River Sink, across the Devil's Playground. Blocked from further movement by the Providence Mountains to the east, the individual grains are then deposited at the dune site.

The tips of desert grasses on the dunes scribe 360-degree arcs with the whirling winds.

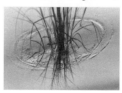

Kelso Dunes are referred to as "booming dunes" for the low vibrational sounds that are created when the sand made of polished grains of rose quartz slides over the underlying surface. The low rumbling sounds emitted by "booming dunes" have been compared to the sound of a chorus or a mythological siren, as well a kettle drum, Tibetan gong or low-flying airplane. Everywhere they occur, from Egypt to Libya to the Kelso Dunes of California, booming dunes have become the stuff of folklore and legend.

The Kelso Dunes may boom, but they still offer hikers plenty of opportunity for solitude and quiet times.

An old story tells of a teamster who started off across the dunes with a wagonload of whiskey to replenish the supplies of the saloons in Kelso. A violent sandstorm arose, and forced the wagonmaster to unhitch his team to wait out the storm. But when he returned to reclaim his property with its important contents, he could not locate it. Legend has it that the sounds that can be heard coming from the dunes on cold, clear nights are really the celebrations of the ghosts of the old teamster and his friends, who have finally located their precious load and are reveling in their discovery.

Since the Kelso Dunes have been closed to off-road vehicles since 1973, they've been relatively protected from the kind of damage that has reduced some of California's dune formations to barren piles of sand.

More than 100 varieties of plants live on or near the dunes, including sand verbena, desert primrose and native grasses. Mesquite and creosote grow on the lower dunes.

Dune-dwelling animals include several species of birds, rodents, sidewinders, lizards and kit foxes. Several insects are found here, and nowhere else in the world, such as the Kelso Dune Jerusalem Cricket.

The dunes are a reminder of nature's power and the never-ending process of change over eons. Photographers and artists attempt to capture the stunning qualities of these dunes, but nothing compares to a first-hand visit.

Prime times to visit the dunes are at daybreak and at sundown. The early morning rays cast a rose-colored glow on the sand, and the fading late afternoon sun gives a bluish-purple appearance. A hike to the crest of the dunes takes two to three hours; plan your trek so you're not out on the dunes during the midday heat. Always bring water and a snack.

The Kelso Dunes provide a fine vantage point from which to gain a stunning view of the preserve. But to get to the top of the shifting sands requires some hard work. Although the hike is short (3 miles round trip with a 400-foot elevation gain), it's somewhat demanding; there's a lot of two step forward, one step back kind of progress, especially as you near the top of the ridge. Take your time, and enjoy the experience; it's not every day you get to play in a giant sandbox.

From Kelso Depot, continue south on Kelbaker Road for 7 miles to a signed dirt road and turn west (right). Drive slowly for 3 miles along this road (navigable for all but very low-slung passenger cars) to a parking area. The trail to the Kelso Dunes begins just up the dirt road from the parking area.

After parking in the designated area, simply head north toward the dunes. Carefully pick your way cross-country. As you near the dunes you'll notice many native grasses growing on the sand.

For further confirmation of the circular pattern of winds that formed the dunes, examine the bunches of grass on the lower slopes. You'll notice that the tips of the tall grasses have etched 360-degree circles on the sand.

Other patterns on the sand are made by the desert's abundant, but rarely seen, wildlife. You might see the tracks of a coyote, kit fox, antelope ground squirrel, packrat, raven or sidewinder. Footprints of lizards and mice can be seen tacking this way and that over the sand. The dune's surface records the lightest pressure of the smallest feet. Only the first quarter-mile or so of the walk to the dunes is on established trail. Once the trail peters out, angle toward the low saddle atop the dunes, just to the right of the highest point.

As you cross the lower dunes, you'll pass some mesquite and creosote bushes. During spring of a good wildflower year, the lower dunes are bedecked with yellow and white desert primrose, pink sand verbena and yellow sunflowers.

When you reach the saddle located to the right of the high point, turn left and trek another hundred yards or so to the top. The black material crowning the top of the dunes is magnetite, an iron oxide, and one of about two dozen minerals found within the dune system.

Enjoy the view from the top: the Kelso Mountains to the north, the Bristol Mountains to the southwest, the Granite Mountains to the south, the Providence Mountains to the east. Everywhere you look there are mountain ranges, small and large. In fact, despite evidence to the contrary—most notably the stunning dunes beneath your feet—this desert is composed mostly of mountains, not sand.

While atop the dunes, perhaps your footsteps will cause mini-avalanches and the dunes will sha-boom-sha-boom for you. There's speculation that the extreme dryness of this desert, combined with the wind-polished, rounded nature of the individual sand grains, has something to do with their musical ability. After picking up good vibrations, descend the steep dune face (much easier on the way down!) and return to the trailhead. While the trek up the mountain of sand might have been slow going, the quick trip down is guaranteed to make you feel like a carefree kid. As you scamper down the dunes with reckless abandon you'll create sand slides and mini-avalanches, and you may hear the characteristic booming sound of the Kelso Dunes as the sand slips across the underlying layer.

13

Granite Mountains

Geologists often call the eastern Mojave a desert of mountains. Most prominent of these many mountains is the chain that trends southwest-northeast across Mojave National Preserve—a high profile combination formed by the Granite, Providence, Mid Hill and New York ranges.

The Granite Mountains, southernmost in the chain, are a little-visited wilderness, the domain of desert big horn sheep. In fact, the craggy shoulders of these 6,000-foot mountains are favored haunts of the elusive creatures.

A lack of asphalt (the sheep refuse to step over paved roads) and scarce human activity in this southern corner of the pre-

serve means a bighorn-friendly environment.

The rugged Granite Mountains—and the preserve's other granite ranges—have been highly eroded; characteristic of this action is the build-up of loose sedimentary materials at the base of the mountains. These apron-shaped formations are called alluvial fans.

Portions of these mountains are part of the University of California's Granite Mountains Natural Reserve. Such reserves represent a wide variety of the state's ecosystems including Big Sur, the Eel River plus a dozen more. UC reserves are dedicated to ecological research and education, and typically serve as outdoor classrooms and field laboratories for students and faculty.

Some 9,000 acres in the Granite Mountains are in the UC reserve, of which 2,500 acres are owned by the University of California. To avoid disturbing any of the natural sciences research projects conducted in the Granite Mountains, please heed the reserve's "No Trespassing" signs and stay on the area's main trails.

SILVER PEAK

At 6,365 feet in elevation, Silver Peak is not the highest summit in the Granite Mountains (that honor belongs to Granite Mountain, the 6,762-foot signature summit located a few miles south of Silver Peak), but it does boast the only semi-decent trail in the range. Rewards for the steep climb to

Silver Peak (8.5 miles round trip with a 2,400-foot elevation gain) are vistas of some of Mojave National Preserve's most famed features including Cima Dome, the Providence Mountains and Kelso Dunes.

The rapid change in elevation along Silver Peak Trail is accompanied by distinct changes in vegetation. At lower elevations in Cottonwood Wash, sage and yucca are among the dominant plants. Higher elevations bring cholla-dotted slopes and then a woodland of pinyon pine and juniper.

Hikers seeking a more modest exploration of the Granite Mountains could hike through Cottonwood Wash two miles or so, and turnaround before the going gets really, really steep.

To reach the trailhead for the Silver Peak trail, exit Interstate 40, about 78 miles east of Barstow and 65 miles west of Needles, on Kelbaker Road and head north into Mojave National Preserve.

Ten miles from I-40, look left (west) for an unsigned dirt road. Actually, two nearly parallel dirt roads (0.3 mile apart) lead westward toward the Granite Mountains and the trailhead. (Clue: another dirt road, nearly opposite the one you're seeking, heads east from the other side of Kelbaker Road.) Those traveling from northern preserve locations on Kelbaker Road, will find the above-mentioned turnoff about 4.6 miles south of the turnoff for Kelso Dunes.

Drive 1.75 miles to a small rise, where there is a camping area (no facilities),

Mojave National Preserve wilderness signs, plus a locked gate and signs forbidding entrance to UC's Granite Mountains preserve.

To begin your adventure, hike west into Cottonwood Wash. After 0.1 mile, the road forks. Stay right and hike up the wash.

Reminders of the area's ranching days come in the form of fencing and dirt tracks leading off to water tanks and corrals.

After about 1.25 miles, the old road narrows to a trail and begins a moderately aggressive ascent up Silver Peak. The path steepens as it passes pinyon pine and juniper. A bit more than three miles out, the trail angles west for 0.5 mile, then north again.

The path ends 0.25 mile and about 300 feet in elevation short of the summit. Cairns help guide you over a very steep and rocky slope to the summit.

14

Providence Mountains

One of the most diverse and certainly most accessible destinations in the eastern Mojave is Providence Mountains State Recreation Area, a 5,900-acre island of state park managed land within the preserve's boundaries. With dramatic mile-high peaks as a backdrop, this area features a variety of plant communities, three short hikes, a small campground, and ranger-led tours of one of the most intriguing limestone caves in the West.

Located off Essex Road, 17 miles north of Interstate 40, this area is a must-see detour for preserve visitors. As you travel north on Essex Road, you'll see the massive Providence Mountains looming to the northwest. The highest peaks in the range

are 6,996-foot Fountain Peak and 7,171-foot Edgar Peak, both located just west of the Providence Mountains State Recreation Area visitor center.

The Providence Mountains, limestone peaks intermixed with ancient volcanic, sedimentary and crystalline formations, are among Mojave's tallest mountains. They rise above the Clipper Valley and Kelso Basin; the west end forms a 600-foot escarpment-one of the most prominent views in this land of basin and range faulting.

During the 1880s, the Bonanza King Mine was a major source of silver in the area. The town of Providence was founded by the miners; its population hovered around 500 until mine operations ceased in 1887. More than 60 million dollars worth of silver was mined from the legendary

Botanic diversity in the Providence Mountains.

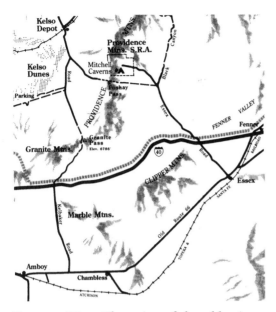

Bonanza King. The ruins of the old mine and the ghost town of Providence can be seen today, but it takes a strenuous rock-climbing adventure to get to them.

These mineral-rich mountains were also the site of a more recent major mining project. During World War II, when demand for iron ore was at an all-time high, the Vulcan Mine, located near Foshay Pass, was operated by Kaiser Steel. More than two million tons of ore were mined here; the mining activity caused a boom in the nearby town of Kelso. But the mine was shut down in 1947, turning Kelso into a virtual ghost town once again.

In 1954, the California state parks system purchased the caves and surrounding land from Ida Mitchell, the widow of Jack Mitchell who developed the area and the caverns that bear his name. Be sure to visit the area's main attraction, Mitchell Caverns, as well as the visitor center and hike one or more of the short trails.

The views in this area are spectacular; from the Overlook Trail near the campground (elevation 4,300 feet) you can see mountains and mesas, valleys and sand dunes. The view of Clipper Valley to the east stretches a hundred open miles. To put that distance in perspective, consider that the entire Los Angeles Basin would fit into the empty valley below. (Then quickly forget such a thought!)

MITCHELL CAVERNS

Jack and Ida Mitchell struck it rich in real estate in Los Angeles in the 1920s. Speculating that there might be a tourism boom in the desert, they staked a claim in the Providence Mountains after learning of the magnificent caverns located in the range. When they lost most of their fortune during the early 1930s, the Mitchells loaded up their Model-T and moved to the desert.

For a time, Jack Mitchell prospected for silver, but his real passion, and that of Ida's, was what the pair called "Providence" or "Crystal" cave. The hard-working couple lived in the caves for nearly a year while they constructed stone accommodations for overnight visitors, built a road and a trail to the caves, staircases and other amenities, intending to attract tourists to the limestone caverns. The hogan-style home they

During the 1930s and 1940s, Jack Mitchell conducted tours through the caverns that now bear his name.

built for themselves is embedded with bits of glass, rocks, gemstones and petrified wood.

Their patience and perseverance paid off, and the visitors began to arrive. The Mitchells led their guests on candle-lit tours of the caverns. By all accounts, Jack Mitchell was quite a yarn-spinner. Some visitors who took his tours way back in the 1930s and 1940s still remember his tall tales of ghosts, lost treasure and bottomless pits.

Stalactites and stalagmites, flowstone and cave shields – hardly what travelers expect to find in arid desert lands.

Now that the caverns are part of the state park system, rangers lead the tours. Stalactites and stalagmites, flowstone, cave spaghetti, cave shields and cave ribbons are among the formations seen in the cool caverns that maintain a constant temperature of 65 degrees year-round. Visitors learn about some of the caverns' former inhabitants—the native Chemehuevi as well as a Pleistocene ground sloth that stumbled into the darkness some 15,000 years ago.

From September through June, you can join a ranger-led tour of the two main chambers, but it's not quite as romantic as it was in the early years. During Jack Mitchell's day, visitors had to be nimble rock climbers and wait for their tour leader to toss flares into the darkness. Nowadays, stairs, railings and electric lights have been installed, and rangers carry flashlights and point out particularly interesting formations. Tour leaders are an enthusiastic, informative lot, and the guided walk (1 to 1.5 miles) is likely to be quite memorable.

California State Park ranger explains the wonders of Mitchell Caverns.

Serious spelunkers can make special arrangements for entrance to Winding Stair Cave.

Guided (fee) tours are conducted Monday through Friday at 1:30 p.m. On Saturday and Sunday, tours begin at 10 a.m., 1:30 p.m. and 3 p.m. A tour takes 1.5 to 2 hours depending on your group's enthusiasm and collective curiosity.

The Mitchells named the two chambers, the first called "El Pakiva," (the Devil's House); the second, "Tecopa," (for a Chemehuevi chieftain). The names are a tribute to the Chemehuevi people, who lived in the caves for nearly 500 years. Anthropologists and archeologists have recovered pottery shards, arrowheads and food caches; they conclude that native people used these caverns, probably on a seasonal basis, for shelter, storage and even certain ceremonies. Young boys were probably left in the darkness of the caves as part of a coming-of-age ritual.

Imagine the life of the Chemeheuvis when they stayed in these caves and mountains. While the men hunted for game, the women tended the children, wove baskets and sandals, and prepared food. When the hunters returned, often loaded with quail, deer and rabbits, the men were enthusiastically welcomed by the rest of the community. After a successful hunt, all celebrated with ritual games and ceremonies; music was an important part of their social activities. Close your eyes a moment and see if you can't conjure up the thin, haunting tones of a four-hole cane flute, the chant of a shaman, the vocal response of the assembled community. These mountains and quiet caverns once reverberated with sound.

The caves were created over several million years. The limestone rock was once the bottom of an ancient ocean; geologic forces uplifted and tilted it high above the body of water. The pressures formed cracks and crevices in the limestone, the very beginning of the cave formation. About 12 million years ago, the earth above the limestone was covered with a thick rain forest. As the saturating rains fell, the rainwater absorbed carbon dioxide from the decomposing plant matter. The slightly acidic water seeped into the cracks and crevices in the limestone and expanded them into caves filled with water.

As the weather changed and became drier over the next several thousand years, the groundwater level lowered, the water-filled caves emptied. When rainfall increased once again, the acidic water seeped into the caves and began depositing a tiny spot of calcite with every drop. Over many thousands of years, the calcite grew into the grand stalactites, stalagmites and other cave formations that can be seen here today.

At present, the caves are not growing; experts speculate that they will eventually—thousands of years from now—weather away and disappear. Because you can only tour the caverns with a park ranger and because you wouldn't want us to spoil the many surprises of the cave walk with a step-by-step description, we won't further detail the Mitchell Caverns tour. However, after exploring "the great indoors" allow some time to explore the preserve's outdoors pathways.

NIÑA MORA TRAIL

Experience the grandeur and isolation of the Providence Mountains, as well as grand vistas, by hiking the short (0.5 mile round trip) Niña Mora Trail. The path ascends the summit of one of a pair of hills known as Camel Humps.

From atop the hump, gaze out over some 300 square miles of desert. Clear-day views include Arizona's Hualapai Mountains, located about 100 miles to the east.

The trail was named for the *niña* (child) Mora, daughter of a Mexican silver miner who toiled in the region's diggings in the early 1900s. A miner's life—as well as that of his family members—was often a short one. And so it was with little Mora, who died at a very early age and lies buried in a grave near the trail that bears her name.

Join the signed path at the east end of the park's tiny campground. From the campground, the path leads over a barrel cactus- and yucca-dotted ridge, and past the grave marker of Niña Mora.

In no time, you reach trail's end and a viewpoint which offers a good perspective on the weathered rhyolite crags of the

Providence Mountains looming to the west. Below is Clipper Valley and to the east is Table Mountain.

CRYSTAL SPRING

Crystal Spring Trail (2 miles round trip with a 600-foot elevation gain) leads into the pinyon pine- and juniper-dotted Providence Mountains by way of Crystal Canyon. Bighorn sheep often travel through this canyon.

Crystal Canyon is walled with limestone and rhyolite, a red volcanic rock. High above the canyon, castle-like formations of this rhyolite crown the Providence Mountains.

The steep and rather rocky trail offers an exploration of an inviting high desert canyon as well as engaging vistas of the spires of Providence Mountains peaks and even a slice of Arizona. Join the signed trail ascending the slope near the beginning of the Mitchell Caverns Trail.

In less than a 0.25-mile ascent, hikers enter a unique desert landscape framed by bold rhyolite outcroppings. Pinyon pine join a veritable cactus garden of barrel, cholla and prickly pear cacti.

About 0.5 mile out, keen-eyed hikers may spy the pipeline Jack Mitchell built in the 1930s to supply his tourist attraction in-the-making. The path crosses to the canyon's right side and continues a last 0.25 mile to the end of the trail, just short of willow-screened Crystal Spring. Intrepid

Naturalist Mary Beal regained her health and recorded a wealth of botanical information when she moved to Mojave.

hikers may proceed on fainter trail to the spring and on to a viewpoint a short distance farther.

MARY BEAL NATURE STUDY TRAIL

Pick up an interpretive booklet from the park visitor center and walk the Mary Beal Nature Trail (0.5-mile round trip), which offers a great introduction to high desert flora. Cliffrose and blue sage share the hillsides with cholla, catclaw and creosote.

The trail honors Mary Beal, a Riverside librarian who was "exiled" to the desert by her doctor for health reasons. For a half-century this remarkable woman wandered through the Providence Mountains and other remote Mojave locales gathering and classifying hundreds of varieties of wildflowers and other plants. The trail was dedicated in 1952 on Beal's seventy-fifth birthday.

Walk the road north of the visitor center to the signed start of the trail.

The path meanders an alluvial plain. Prickly pear, cholla and assorted yuccas spike surrounding slopes. Benches offer restful places from which to contemplate the cacti, admire the volcanic boulders and count the speedy roadrunners often seem scurrying across the trail. Also savor views of the Providence Mountains and of Clipper Valley.

15

Mid Hills & Hole-in-the-Wall

Mojave's central area, highlighted by two popular camping areas at Mid Hills and Hole-in-the-Wall, is characterized by its high elevation, classic basin-and-range terrain (flattop peaks separated by dry valleys), unusual volcanic rock formations and outstanding views of the surrounding sandscape.

The pinyon pine-juniper woodland flourishes in the high elevations of the preserve. Visitors find it a welcome sight to view large trees in the middle of the desert. The trees provide shade, and the elevation ensures cooler temperatures than those found in the surrounding lower desert. It's one of the few places in the preserve where mid-summer camping can be considered;

daytime temperatures usually reach only into the 90s. In the winter, however, snowstorms are common, while springtime usually brings colorful blooms. Snow flurries and hail, although unusual, may occur into mid-May.

Driving to the region on Black Canyon Road, you'll note the magnificent Providence Mountains to the west, and in the distance, the smaller Kelso and Marl Ranges. To the east are the steep Woods Mountains and one of the preserve's most distinctive landmarks, Table Mountain, a 6,176-foot mesa that juts up from the desert floor. It can be seen from many vantage points throughout Mojave, despite its close proximity to other great mountains—the Providence range to the southwest and the New York Mountains to the north. As your drive closer, the mountain's white granite base topped by dark lava cliffs is an impressive sight.

This is open country, reminiscent of the Old West, complete with barbed wire fences, sagebrush, range cattle, occasional windmills, and views that go on forever.

Hikers can ascend to the summit of steep-sided Table Mountain via a route that's about one-third dirt road and two-thirds cross-country travel. Reward for the 3.5-mile one-way climb (with 1,000 foot elevation gain) to the top of the flat-topped mesa is a 360-degree panoramic view of much of the preserve.

To reach the trailhead for the Table

Tabletop mesas abound in this basin-and-range geology of Mojave National Preserve.

Mountain climb, head 6.4 miles south on Black Canyon Road from its junction with Cedar Canyon Road. Park on the east side of the road and look for the trail (an old dirt road) that begins on the northeast side of the parking area.

The path leads east a mile, then north to a windmill and water tank. Then you head for the mountain by way of two eastward approaches—either by way of a ridge or by hiking along the base of the ridge.

Wild Horse Canyon Road, which loops from Hole-in-the-Wall Campground to Mid Hills Campground, was declared the nation's first official "Back Country By-way" in 1989 when the U.S. Bureau of Land Management administered the area. Anyone who drives the eleven-mile, horse-

Scenic Wild Horse Canyon Road from Mid Hills to Hole-in-the-Wall: America's first official "Back Country Byway."

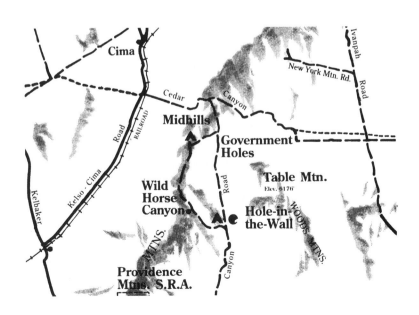

Pointing out a few of the sights in this classic devil's garden located in Wildhorse Canyon.

shoe-shaped road will agree that it's worthy of this honor and any other awards bestowed on America's most scenic routes.

Beginning at Hole-in-the-Wall, Wild Horse Canyon Road crosses wide-open country dotted with cholla and, in season, delicate purple, yellow, white and red wildflowers. Dramatic volcanic slopes and flat-top mesas tower over this low desert. Proceeding northward, visitors will encounter a landscape of sagebrush, then inviting pinyon-juniper woodland.

The road takes travelers from the 4,200-foot level at Hole-in-the-Wall to mile-high Mid Hills Campground. In fact, one of the attractions of the road is the diversity of scenery that changes with the elevation. If you're very lucky, you'll spot deer or even a bighorn sheep on the rocky slopes above the road.

MID HILLS

Two miles west of Black Canyon Road, this campground is located in pinyon pine-juniper woodland and offers outstanding views. This mile-high place, filled with sagebrush and piles of granite rock, resembles the Great Basin Desert of Nevada and Utah.

Mid Hills, so named because of its location midway between the Providence and New York Mountains, is a unique vantage point from which to observe Mojave's largest and most distinctive ranges. To the north, can be seen the cappuccino-colored

Three of Mojave's most prominent plants: cholla, yucca, and Joshua tree.

Pinto Mountain, to the west lie the rolling Kelso Sand Dunes.

The isolated campground's central location offers two major features that appeal to those wanting to "get away from it all." It's easy to reach, yet it feels like it's miles from nowhere. With more than two dozen well-spaced campsites and recently up-graded facilities, it allows visitors a sense of privacy, while incorporating a feeling of campground community. At the north end of the campground, looking northwest, is the preserve's best view of Cima Dome, the 75-square-mile formation of uplifted once-molten rock.

"Dromedary Rock," located near Mid Hills

One of the most intriguing aspects of the Mid Hills area is the dominant plant life—the pinyon pine-juniper forest. During Pleistocene times, a few hundred thousand years ago, these cone-bearing trees flourished throughout the Mojave. As the weather became more and more arid, the range of these trees was restricted to higher elevations, which provided sufficient precipitation for their growth.

The tall, fragrant, two-needle pines that are so prominent in this area were once an important food source. In the fall, when the nuts were ripe and most plentiful, the Chemehuevi, Piute, and other native people, traveled to the places where the sturdy cone-bearing trees lived. They broke the pinecones off the trees, then roasted them to gather the nuts hidden inside.

Today, hungry hikers enjoy collecting

Mid Hills often seems as if it's in the middle of nowhere.

the creamy-white nuts; their tangy, vaguely piney taste makes an interesting trailside snack. But be sure to take a few home; pinenuts (also known as pignolas) are delicious when added to a salad, or sprinkled atop pasta tossed with pesto sauce.

The small, twisted juniper tree is the other dominant plant of this area. This unique pine bears distinctive blue berries in the spring; they are the source from which gin is made.

Also thriving in this area is the low sagebrush scrub community, with its pungently fragrant sage, assorted cacti, and springtime wildflowers.

MID HILLS TO HOLE-IN-THE-WALL HIKE

The hiking trail linking Mid Hills Campground with Hole-in-the-Wall, eight miles to the south, is the preserve's longest, as well as best signed and maintained trail. The path was constructed in the late 1980s by the California Conservation Corps.

Mid Hills is a thousand feet or so higher in elevation than Hole-in-the-Wall; thus, most hikers choose the "downhill" route and begin their journey at Mid Hills. The hike is a bit more than eight miles one-way with a 1,000-foot elevation loss.

It's an adventurous undertaking through a diverse desert environment. You'll see piles of rounded boulders at the northern end, basin and range tabletop mesas at the southern end of the trail. Along the way, you'll encounter large pinyon trees, an array of colorful cactus and lichen-covered granite rocks. The views of Table Mountain, Wild Horse Mesa and the Providence Range are unparalleled.

A word about desert hiking in general and this desert hike in particular: You'll often travel in the bottom of sandy washes instead of over more clearly defined trails found in forest locales. This means the hiker

The eight-mile, mostly down-hill route between Mid Hills and Hole-in-the-Wall is a memorable hike.

must rely on maps, a sense of direction, rock cairns and the very occasional sign.

To reach the Mid Hills trailhead, take the signed turnoff from Black Canyon Road and travel two miles to the campground. The Mid Hills trailhead is located adjacent to a windmill immediately opposite the entrance road to the campground.

In a short distance, the path ascends to a saddle which offers splendid views of the Pinto Valley to the northeast. (The saddle is this hike's high point.)

From the saddle, the path angles south, descending into, then climbing out of a wash. (Keep a close eye on the trail; it's a bit tricky here.) The trail reaches a dirt road, follows it for a mere 100 feet, then turns sharply left to join a wash for a time, exits it, and crosses a road. You encounter another wash, enter it and exit it.

After a modest ascent, the trail joins a road, passes through a gate, and joins another road for a little more than a mile. This road serves up spectacular views to the south of the Providence Mountains and Wild Horse Mesa.

Adjacent to a group of large boulders, a road veers left but hikers bear right, soon turning sharp left with the road. The route passes through another gate, then works its way through a dense thicket of cholla cactus.

After following another wash, the trail crosses a dirt road, then soon joins a second road, which follows a wash to a dead end at an abandoned dam. The trail ascends through some rocks, levels for a time, then descends. A quarter mile before trail's end, you'll spy the Hole-in-the-Wall spur trail leading off to the left. Climb the rings and steep pathway up to Hole-in-the-Wall.

HOLE-IN-THE-WALL

Hole-in-the-Wall is an inviting locale, the kind of place Butch Cassidy and the Sundance Kid would choose as a hideout. A fine camping area (named one of the top 100 campgrounds in the west by *Sunset* magazine) and an unforgettable hiking experience attract visitors.

Directly east of the campground are the Woods Mountains. The range features appropriately named Rustlers Canyon, an out-of-the way place where cattle rustlers and various outlaws once hid out from lawmen.

Although the location of the small campground at Hole-in-the-Wall (elevation 4,200 feet) is pleasant enough to attract campers, bird-watchers and others who just want to "stay-put," more adventurous types find the highlight of a trip to Hole-in-the-Wall is exploring the wondrous volcanic formations that form its backdrop. Visit the Information Center (at present, not regularly staffed) located here.

Immediately west of the campground is a maze of volcanic rocks that descend first into Banshee Canyon, then into a large, open desert box canyon named Wildhorse Canyon. The two canyons couldn't be more

Hole-in-the-Wall
Visitor Center

dissimilar; they provide the visitor with a glimpse of the diversity of the Mojave National Preserve.

Hikers once used ropes and ladders to descend into Banshee Canyon from the campground area; today the descent is accomplished by negotiating two sets of iron rings that have been set into the rock. Maneuvering through the rings is not particularly difficult for those who are reasonably agile and take their time. But acrophobes or claustrophobes may want to pass on this adventure.

Walter Ford, in a 1941 article published in *Desert* magazine, recounted his experiences in Hole-in-the-Wall: "With a 100-foot rope securely tied around a large boulder I crawled over the over-hanging ledge and found myself dangling in mid-air with the next projecting rock 25 feet below! We had assumed that there would be footholds all the way down but here was a condition with which we had not reckoned. Hastily throwing a couple of turns of rope around one of my legs, I let myself drop hand-over-hand to the rock below. From that point I could see that the remaining distance would be over steep, sandstone slopes with few footholds anywhere. Playing out the rope as I went I began a series of zigzags only to find that my momentum increased as I descended. When about 10 feet from the bottom the rope slipped from my grasp and I landed in a heap at the bottom."

Fortunately for today's hiker, the descent

on iron rings is nowhere near as harrowing as it once was. Just remember the old rock climber's adage: secure three limbs before moving the fourth.

The story about the naming of Hole-in-the-Wall is easy to envision as you encounter the twisted maze of red rock. As

Co-author Cheri Rae explores Hole-in-the-Wall.

the legend goes, in the 1880s, a couple of ranch hands from nearby Dominguez Ranch were searching for some stray cattle, and they came upon a pair of Indians who were leading a few cattle. Suspecting them of stealing their stock, the ranch hands chased the Indians into a canyon, which they thought was a deadend. To their amazement, the Indians scrambled up the rocks in the lower canyon, and then disappeared—seemingly right into the blank wall. The men concluded the Indians must have found or created a hole in the wall.

Enjoy exploring the volcanic rock formations known as rhyolite, a crystallized form of lava. The holes provide frames for taking silly photographs. You might spot any number of raptors circling overhead: golden eagles, hawks and owls.

Hole-in-the-Wall rocks have a violent past—geologically speaking, that is. Some 18 million years ago, a volcano in the Woods Mountains erupted and spewed ash and rocks (some 60 feet across—among the largest ever documented!). Hot ashes cremated every living thing in the area; countless plant and animal fossils lie entombed beneath the volcanic tuff of Hole-in-the-Wall's cliffs.

To reach the trailhead for the Hole-in-the-Wall hike (a two-mile round trip excursion), follow the dirt road past the visitor center to the parking area at the picnic ground. The path plunges into a wall of rocks. Grasp the iron rings and lower yourself into Banshee Canyon. Descend amidst the impressive pock-marked canyon walls. You can turn around at the canyon bottom or continue as your route curves north toward Wild Horse Canyon.

Hole-in-the-Wall is not the only place in this area with a colorful name. Banshee is named not for the shrieking elves of the Scottish Highlands, but for the sounds said to be heard here at night that resemble their cries. Horned owls and the sound of the wind whistling through the holes make a quiet night in the canyon unlikely.

You can extend your hike through Banshee Canyon that in turn leads to Wild Horse Canyon. Follow Banshee to its opening, then turn north follow the wash and pick your way cross-country to the indistinct trail leading northward. The trail climbs gently onto a low mesa that offers good views of Wild Horse Mesa to the left, and desert varnish-covered rock formations on the right.

Continue northward through a magnificent devil's garden filled with yucca, cholla, beavertail, barrel and prickly pear cactus. In the springtime, the cactus bloom spreads bright yellow and hot pink across the canyon.

As you near the end of the canyon, enjoy the view of the juniper-filled basin to the north, the mountains and mesas in every direction. If you continued northward, you would reach Mid Hills, but the hike between the two campgrounds is best done north to south.

16

Lanfair Valley

Driving north on Lanfair Road from the small town of Goffs, you'll view a wide-open landscape of yucca and Joshua trees, with several mountain ranges in the distance. There's hardly a trace of the early-20th-century farming community that once stood here. The intersection of Cedar Canyon and Lanfair Roads was once the entrance to a small town populated by farmers and ranchers.

Homesteaders descended on the Mojave Desert during America's period of westward expansion, from 1860 through 1920. Not coincidentally, this was also a period of particularly wet weather in the Mojave. Cattle ranchers and farmers settled in with varied success, but they gave their new homesteads optimistic names such as Golden, Surprise and Superior.

Edwin Lanfair lent his name to the area originally named Paradise Valley after he settled in 1910. The valley's first successful farmer, Lanfair raised bumper crops of wheat and barley in the desert. His good fortune attracted other homesteaders who flocked to the area; some managed to grow enough produce to sell it in markets in Needles.

The shortage of water was an ever-present problem in the valley. Although two wells were eventually established by

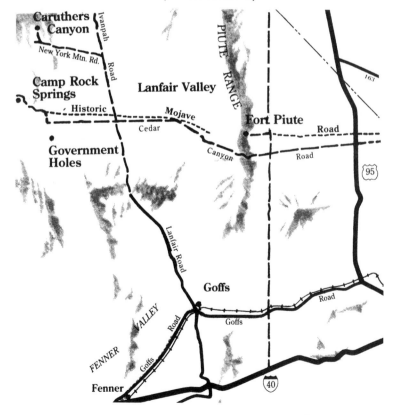

Ranch in Ivanpah
District, circa 1880.

Lanfair, many homesteaders chose instead to transport their water from Government Holes, a dozen miles to the west. The continued mild, wet weather held, encouraging them to stay, despite the difficulty of eking out a living in the middle of the desert.

The ranchers who had lived in the area were unhappy with the burgeoning homestead community. They refused to sell the farmers even a drop of water. Long-simmering disputes over land and water rights developed between small farmers, ranchers and big cattlemen. They finally erupted in a Wild West shootout at Government Holes.

Earlier, a few homesteaders infuriated Rock Springs cattle ranchers when they purchased several head of sheep and cattle and began grazing them on the open range. Considering this act an infringement on their grazing rights, the ranchers eventually fenced off the water supply at Government Holes, the only dependable source of water available to the homesteaders.

The already tense situation became even worse when hot tempers flared between a former Rock Springs man turned homesteader Matt Burts, a convicted train robber, and J.W. Robinson, the newly hired Rock Springs foreman, known for his shady, violent past.

When Burts offered to drive his friend R.L. Fulton to work, the radiator of his car began leaking. He nursed the vehicle toward Government Holes, where he intended to get some water. When he called out and announced his plan, Robinson told him to go ahead; when Burts finished filling the radiator, he approached the cabin to talk with Robinson. Shots rang out and when Fulton ran in, he found both men mortally wounded. Apparently, Robinson had ambushed Burts, who then pulled his gun and killed Robinson as he fell to the floor.

This 1925 duel was the final blow for the homestead community of Lanfair Valley. Two years prior to the incident at Government Holes, the Nevada Southern Railroad abandoned the station it had established in Lanfair Valley to handle the ores shipped from local mines. A decline in mining activity and a debilitating strike were the reasons cited for the closure.

The end of the railroad, the onset of a period of increasingly arid weather, and the homesteaders' loss of confidence in the community after the violence at Government Holes all contributed to the end of the settlement. In 1926, the store and post office were closed.

Although ranchers still graze their herds in Lanfair Valley, few traces remain of the earlier settlers. A windmill here, a water tank there, and some ruins are all that remain of the the original settlements—reminders of the dreams of optimistic homesteaders whose hopes were dashed by the harsh realities of desert life.

DUNBAR

The Lanfair Valley town of Dunbar was founded in 1911 by G.W. Harts, Howard Folkes, and other enterprising African-Americans. The community, which numbered some 20 families, tried to cultivate cotton, and intended to build an industrial training school for orphans. The harsh desert environment defeated the town's agricultural efforts and thwarted the other good works of these pioneers. Dunbar lasted only three years before the post office closed and its residents abandoned the town.

FORT PIUTE

Fort Piute is nestled in the Piute Range, with a grand view all the way to Arizona, and next to the dependable water source at Piute Creek. It's easy to imagine the despair felt by the tiny contingent of soldiers assigned to this desolate spot.

Fort Piute is located east of Lanfair Valley, at the southern end of the Piute Mountains. It was established in the 1860s as one of a chain of five outposts along the Government Road—stretching from Fort Mojave in Nevada to Camp Cady to the west—to provide a military presence in the desert, and to protect pioneer travelers on their westward journeys.

As was the case in much of the West, Indians resisted the intrusion of settlers on their tribal lands. There were frequent attacks on westbound settlers and mail wag-

The isolated ruins of
Fort Piute.

ons traveling the route from Prescott, Arizona, to Los Angeles.

The military escorts presumably protected the travelers, but the conditions at the outpost were intolerable for many soldiers at Fort Piute. Desertion was a regular occurrence, and the outpost was officially staffed by just 18 men of the Company "D" 9th Infantry Division from 1867 to 1868.

Fort Piute was described by visitor Elliot Coues as "a Godforsaken Botany Bay of a place—the meanest I ever saw for a military station." It's doubtful that many who visit this tiny, lonely Army outpost would disagree.

Originally named Fort Beale, for Edward F. Beale who led his camels through this area, the outpost was renamed Fort Piute in 1866. Today the small, primitive installation lies in ruins; its thick rock and mortar walls have been weathered and crumbled to a height of just two or three feet. The stone outlines of the original buildings delineate three connecting rooms that served as a tiny living quarters, corral and cookhouse.

Near the fort stands an early example of an Army make-work project that dates back more than a century. The popular tale is that the rock wall situated above Piute Creek was constructed by Army troops who were then instructed to tear it down and rebuild it on the same site. No doubt the project kept several soldiers busy for some time.

There are many petroglyphs located near Fort Piute—evidence of the presence of native people long before the outpost was established. Soldiers who passed through the area in the mid-1800s sketched their versions of the artifacts. Look for them and try to determine the meaning and significance of the interesting shapes and figures. Although they have been studied extensively, they are still not completely understood.

Visitor points out ruts made by wagons traveling the Mojave Road.

THE OLD MOJAVE ROAD

The Mojave Road was a major trade and transportation route between Arizona and the coast. One look at the rough road gives you an idea of the hardships experienced by the pioneers who passed this way 130 years ago. Piute Hill, on the Mojave Road, was said to be among the most feared obstacles of the westward crossing. In 1867, Brigadier General James F. Rusling described the ordeal of crossing the hill as "the worst climb I encountered in my entire tour across the continent."

What messages do these markings convey?

As they pushed and pulled and dragged their heavy wagons up the rocky hills, the weary travelers prodded their oxen to keep them moving. Sometimes they were forced to wedge lumber beneath the wheels as they struggled to prevent the wagons from rolling backward, pouring every ounce of strength into creating forward momentum. Their taxing effort finally got them over the treacherous pass. But as the pioneers worked and maneuvered their cumbersome loads, the wagon wheels slowly ground into the surface of the rock. Over time, the wagonloads carved deep ruts in the solid rock; these ruts are still visible on Piute Hill today. They remain as vivid reminders of the difficulties faced—and overcome—by determined men and women of another age.

Today, four-wheel-drive enthusiasts still use the Mojave Road but they take a slightly different route than early travelers. Now the road is more apt to be seen as recreation, not desperation.

PIUTE VALLEY AND PIUTE CREEK

The only perennial stream in the preserve, Piute Creek is an oasis-like area where cottonwoods, willows and sedges flourish. Bighorn sheep frequently visit this watering site, as do a large number of birds. Indians once farmed pumpkins, corn,

The thick willows and cottonwoods lining Piute Creek pose a challenge for hikers.

melons and other crops near the spring, and others diverted its flow and irrigated their fields.

Access to the water and the rich hunting and farming land of the surrounding area was once hotly disputed between local Indian tribes. This idyllic location was also the location of a series of horrifying battles between Indians and westward travelers, including soldiers and trappers. In 1827, Jedediah Smith and the remainder of his party holed up near here after ten of his fellow trappers were killed, and in 1859 at least twenty men died in a bloody confrontation.

In more recent years, enterprising George Irwin established a turkey ranch near here; a few remains of the ranch can still be seen east of the creek.

Although the creek has been a dependable source of water for centuries, the water is no longer safe to drink. Don't be tempted, or you'll pay for it later.

FORT PIUTE HIKE

The hike to Fort Piute (6.5 miles round trip with a 600-foot elevation gain) explores Piute Creek and gorge and gives you a chance to walk a portion of the historic Mojave Road. Following the Mojave Road Trail, as its called, lets you walk back into time and get a glimpse of the hardships faced by early pioneers.

This is not a hike for the inexperienced or for first-time visitors to the area; the roads and paths are unsigned and sometimes

Piute Gorge – magnificent when viewed from both far and near.

hard to follow. Experienced hikers and repeat visitors, however, will thoroughly enjoy their exploration of Fort Piute.

To reach the trailhead for the hike to Fort Piute, head west on Interstate 40 and take the turnoff for the road leading to the hamlet of Goffs. Pass through Goffs and drive some 16 miles along Lanfair Road to a point about 100 feet beyond its junction with Cedar Canyon Road. Turn right (east) on a road that goes by four names: Cedar Canyon Road, the utility road, Cable Road, Pole Road. The latter three names arise from the fact that the road follows a buried telephone cable. Drive east, staying right at a junction 3.7 miles out, and sticking with the cable road about 6 more miles to another junction where there's a cattle guard. Turn left before the cattleguard on another dirt road and proceed 0.5 mile to an intersection with an abandoned section of the Mojave Road.

From the intersection of Lanfair and Cedar Canyon Roads, drive east on the utility road 9.5 miles. Turn north on small dirt road that leads 0.5 mile to the old Mojave Road.

(Fort Piute is also accessible from the east, but it's four-wheel drive access only. Turn west off US 95 at milepost 75, north of Goffs Road. Use caution; the road is rough and potholed.)

Begin your trek at Piute Hill and a meeting with the old Mojave Road just over the crest of the hill. From atop the hill, pause to take in the view. Table Mountain can be seen directly to the west, and in the north are Castle Peaks.

Happily for hikers, the route leads down the difficult grade that challenged early pioneers. No doubt the volcanic rock on the road really rattled the settlers' wagons.

On the two miles of travel on Mojave Road, you'll pass along loose, sandy trail near Piute Creek, where there's nice picnicking. (The water in the creek is not safe to drink.) To avoid trampling the creekbed, try taking the trail on the north side of the creek.

About 0.5 mile from the fort, you'll cross the creek. The Mojave Road narrows. Look sharply for the Piute Canyon Trail coming in from the west. (This will be your optional return route.) Continue on a slight descent to the fort.

An interpretive marker provides some historic information about the history of "Fort Pah Ute, 1867-68." Don't sit on the walls or disturb the ruins; like all cultural resources in the desert, the fort is protected by federal law.

Head back along the Mojave Road 0.5-mile, bearing right on unsigned Piute Canyon Trail. This narrow path stays high on the canyon wall, heading west at first, then north. A half-mile along, you can see prominent Piute Gorge to the west; you'll be following this gorge back to the trailhead.

The trail is very faint; if you lose the

path, keep heading west and descending to the floor of Piute Gorge. Expect a steep scramble to reach the bottom of the gorge.

At the bottom, you'll proceed west up Piute Gorge; stay on the gorge bottom. After a half-mile you'll come to an intersection where another canyon comes in from the left. Don't take this route, but continue up the gorge to the right.

A little farther, a trail leading out of the gorge takes off from the left. (Keep a sharp eye out for this one.) Take this trail up to the rim of the gorge, where there's a scenic overlook. From here, follow the dirt road south past a corral back to the trailhead.

17

New York Mountains

ounded by Cima Road on the west
and Cedar Canyon to the south are
the New York Mountains. The
granite peaks of the range are the most
prominent feature in the northeast corner
of the preserve. This is a land of mountain-
tops and canyons, unique botanical communities and fascinating geology.

Thrusting high above Lanfair Valley, the
impressive, granite-crowned New York
Mountains are among the preserve's highest
peaks. New York Peak, the range's 7,463-
foot signature summit, offers commanding
views of the preserve and far beyond—
to the Panamint Mountains of Death Valley
National Park, the San Jacinto Mountains
behind Palm Springs, as well as the moun-

tains of Nevada and western Arizona.

The steep range of granite and limestone also features a number of volcanic formations, including walls of lava on Pinto Mountain (elevation 6,144 feet). Castle Peaks, jagged red-colored volcanic spires composed of andesite are quite prominent, even when viewed from Fort Piute, across Lanfair Valley, and from other faraway locales.

Some 300 plant species have been counted on the slopes of this range and in such colorfully named canyons as Cottonwood, Cliff, Butcher Knife and Fourth of July. Botanists have even discovered several species of ferns here, some of which are found nowhere else. In addition to these individual species, there are some unique botanical communities in the New York

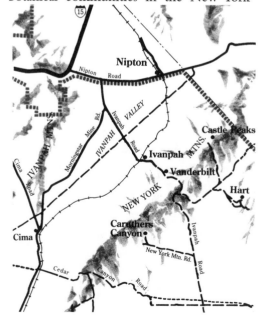

Mountains area; experts refer to them as disjuncts. The isolated communities of pinyon pine and white fir, along with coastal chaparral plants grew throughout this area during wetter times. As the weather became more arid, the coastal and mountain ecosystems were "stranded," and they managed to survive to this day. A white fir forest stands near the top of New York Mountain; pinyon pine and juniper woodlands are found above 4,000 feet throughout the area; a coastal chaparral community thrives at Caruthers Canyon. Discovering the area's colorful history is another attraction of driving and hiking in the New York Mountains.

Visitors will note several man-made features—signs and fences, homesteads and water tanks—clues that miners and ranchers make a living off this land. But few clues remain—mostly abandoned mines and ghost town ruins far up into the hills—to tell the story of the way of life that once

All aboard! Everyone who lived and worked in Mojave counted on the railroad.

boomed here. The hills come alive, however, with a reading of the colorful tales of the area's bad guys and lawmen, chivalrous duels and lost mines.

Mojave National Preserve and Automobile Club maps still show the townsites of Vanderbilt, Barnwell and Hart. As you drive through the New York Mountains on Ivanpah Road or Hart Mine Road, try to imagine what Mojave life was like during this bygone era.

VANDERBILT

Gold miners who staked claims here in 1890 dubbed their new town Vanderbilt in honor of the wealthy industrialist Commodore Cornelius Vanderbilt. The miners figured the name would bring fame, fortune and prestige—not to mention a good deal of luck. By the dawn of the 20th century, the town's population reached 3,000 and boasted a weekly newspaper, several general stores and saloons, a few boarding houses and a number of social clubs. It takes some imagination to conjure up the vision, but the citizens of this one-time boomtown created their own theatrical company, orchestra and even a literary society.

One of the area's movers and shakers was Isaac Blake, who made his fortune with Standard Oil and purchased a smelting plant in Needles and interests in several area mining projects. In 1892, he began construction of the Nevada Southern, a private railroad in the Providence Moun-

Vanderbilt, Barnwell, and Lanfair have faded away, but back in 1920 the towns were big enough for regularly scheduled rail service.

tains. A few years later, he built the California and Eastern Railroad, a narrow gauge line that ran between Vanderbilt and Ivanpah Dry Lake. The railroads enabled miners to ship ore to waiting markets, and the town prospered.

After an initial boom, when the area mines —Gold Bar, Gold Bronze and Boomerang—combined to produce more than two million turn-of-the-century dollars worth of gold, the town's prosperity waned. The low-grade gold required extensive and expensive processing. Mine operators soon realized they could not turn a profit when they added up the high production costs.

Townspeople, always concerned about the unreliable water supply, were faced with the fact that gold mining was no longer dependable either. As was the case with so many other boomtowns, Vanderbilt soon became yet another ghost town, its buildings and the possessions of its former residents taken over by time. Today, only a few ruins of the old buildings remain here.

Mining camp, New York Mountains.

MANVEL (BARNWELL)

Another small town, originally known as Manvel (later Barnwell), was once located four miles south of Vanderbilt. Not a mining town, but a railroad camp, the late 19th-century settlement was a major drop-off point for products shipped from Needles and Goffs on their way to the small mining camps and settlements nearby—including the then-tiny town of Las Vegas, Nevada.

When bypassed by the large San Pedro, Los Angeles and Salt Lake Railroad, the town quietly folded.

The last of the town's original settlers was Dick Diamond, a former slave who moved to Manvel in the 1890s. Diamond, who lived to the age of 100, died in 1950. As the story goes, for the sixty years he lived in Manvel, Diamond proudly displayed a lithograph of Abraham Lincoln on his living room wall, explaining to all his visitors that it was Lincoln who had made him a free man. Like many other mining towns, Barnwell has been reduced to ruins.

HART

The town of Hart is still found on some modern maps. Blink and you'll miss it. Hart was established when gold was discovered in 1907. Less than a year later, the town had a newspaper, two hotels and eight saloons, a small population of miners and several mines, none of which recouped initial investment costs.

An old miner, Stoney Feetham, who operated out of Hart, is said to have found a remarkably rich vein of gold in the hills not far out of town. Greedily, he stuffed his pockets, the bags carried by his burro, and every other container with as much gold-filled ore as he could carry. He quickly hatched a plan to hide his booty and return to the site to mine it in earnest. Back in Hart, Feetham told no one of his discovery. When he went back to mine the vein again, he couldn't even find a trace of it. When they finally found out about his so-called vein, Feetham was ridiculed by his friends, who derisively referred to it as the "Lost Mine of the Clouds." For the rest of his life, Old Stoney searched for "his" gold. He never found it.

The mines were no longer productive by the time the town was virtually destroyed by fire in 1910, but a few hopefuls hung on until the last mine finally closed in 1918. In the town's later years, the pressures of economic losses, along with the stresses of living in an isolated, harsh environment, began to take their toll.

In 1913, the town was a site of an impassioned argument that ended in a shoot-out between two miners who were fighting over the attentions of a local woman. One shot the other, then, feeling immediately remorseful about his deed, sought medical attention for his dying rival, and turned himself in to the sheriff at Goffs. The gunman was jailed, the other man died.

Fenced-off areas, heavy machinery, and trucks rumbling through the New York Mountains are clues to visitors that mining and milling continue today among many of the sites where prospectors once trudged, loaded with pickaxe and hopeful hearts.

CARUTHERS CANYON

Located just a short hike off New York Mountain Road, Caruthers Canyon is a quiet retreat nestled in the New York Range.

Hikers, birdwatchers and botany buffs enjoy exploring Caruthers Canyon. It's a popular campsite (no facilities).

Caruthers Canyon is surely one of the most botanically unique areas in the preserve. A cool, inviting pinyon pine-juniper woodland stands in marked contrast to the sparsely vegetated sandscape common in other parts of the desert. The conifers are joined by oaks and a variety of coastal chaparral plants including manzanita, yerba santa, ceanothus and coffee berry. What is a coastal ecosystem doing in the middle of the desert?

Botanists believe that during wetter times such coastal scrub vegetation was quite widespread. As the climate became more arid, coastal ecosystems were "stranded" atop high and moist slopes. The botanical islands high in the New York Mountains are outposts of Rocky Mountains and coastal California flora. Botanists call them disjuncts. Bureaucrats call them UPAs (Unusual Plant Assemblages). The more lyrical naturalists among us call them islands on the land.

Great birdwatching opportunities abound in the woodland community: Enthusiasts may spot Western tanager, gray-headed junco, yellow breasted chat, and a number of raptors, including golden eagles, prairie falcons and red-tailed hawks.

Caruthers Canyon is a treat for the hiker. An abandoned dirt road provides a short hike (3 miles round trip with a 400-foot elevation gain) that leads through a rocky basin and into a historic gold mining

Pinyon pines, great granite boulders, and clean fresh air.

Abandoned mine shafts, like this one in Caruthers Canyon, abound in the Mojave. Contemplate the dreams that built them, but don't venture into the dark, unsafe passages.

region. Prospectors began digging in the New York Mountains in the 1860s and continued well into the 20th century. At trail's end are a couple of mine shafts.

The drive to Caruthers Canyon is well worth the effort. From its junction with Ivanpah Road, head west on New York Mountains Road. A couple ranch buildings stand near this road's intersection with Ivanpah Road. Drive 5.5 miles to an unsigned junction with a dirt road and turn north. Proceed 2 miles to a woodland laced with turnouts that serve as unofficial campsites. Leave your car here; farther along the road dips into a wash and gets very rough.

From the Caruthers Canyon "campground" follow the main dirt road up the canyon. As you ascend, look behind you for a great view of Table Mountain.

Handsome boulders line the trail and frame views of the tall peak before you, New York Mountain. The range's 7,532-foot signature peak is crowned with a botanical island of its own-a relict stand of Rocky Mountain white fir.

A half-mile along, you'll come to a fork in the road. The rightward road climbs 0.25 mile to an old mining shack. Take the left fork, dipping in and out of a wash and gaining a great view of the canyon.

If it's rained recently, you might find water collected in pools on the rocky canyon bottom. Enjoy the tranquility of the gold mine area, but don't stray into the dark, dangerous shafts.

KEYSTONE CANYON

Keystone Canyon shares botanical similarities with Caruthers Canyon, located a few miles to the south. Both canyons cradle relict stands of white fir—arboreal survivors from a time of much cooler and wetter climatic conditions.

While the last Ice Age evaporated some 10,000 years ago and the Mojave has become a considerably drier landscape, the firs and "coastal" flora still flourish. The survival of these moist-environment plants in the New York Mountains is due to the ranges height; the high peaks snag moisture from passing storms and clouds.

The high elevation-dwelling firs are by no means the only attraction for tree-lovers along the Keystone Canyon Trail. Lower Keystone Canyon hosts pinyon pine, juniper and turbinella oak. More typical preserve vegetation such as Mojave yucca, sagebrush and prickly pear are also present.

From Keystone Canyon the hike to road's end is 3 miles round trip with a 700-foot elevation gain. Hikers bound for the top of New York Peak face a 4.5 mile round trip with a 2,000-foot elevation gain.

Seasoned hikers with good route-finding skills will most enjoy the steep and challenging ascent to New York Peak. (Experienced desert peak-baggers ascend via a couple different routes, including a scramble by way of Keystone Spring.) Those hikers seeking an easier outing can traverse fascinating Keystone Canyon and turn around at road's end.

While the view from atop New York Peak is unsurpassed, hikers be warned that some serious rock scrambling is required to reach the summit. However, nearly the same glorious panorama is available from the ridgecrest below the peak.

To reach Keystone Canyon and the trailhead for the hike to New York Peak, exit on Nipton Road from I-15 and travel 3.5 miles to Ivanpah Road. Turn right (south) and head toward the New York Mountains. Twelve miles along, the road crosses railroad tracks, bends east, and turns to dirt. After six more miles, just as dirt Ivanpah Road bends southeast, turn right on the narrow, unsigned road leading to Keystone Canyon. Avoid a couple left-forking, narrower roads, and travel 2.5 miles from Ivanpah Road to a junction just before the road descends into Keystone Canyon. Briefly follow the left fork to a parking area.

Walk up the deteriorating road into Keystone Canyon. The wide range of trailside flora includes pinyon pine and juniper, yerba santa and cliffrose.

Keystone Canyon bends south and you'll stick with it. A half-mile out, ignore a right-forking road that leads into Live Oak Canyon, and after another 0.1 mile, ignore a left-forking road; this one leads 0.25 mile to Keystone Spring.

Continue your ascent through Keystone Canyon as the views of granite-topped mountains improve and the road you're following gets worse. At road's end, about 1.5

miles from the trailhead, you'll find a small abandoned copper mine. It's colorful in an odd sort of way—green and blue copper ore debris scattered around the mine shaft.

Above you to the southwest are two gullies leading toward the crest. Choose one of them and begin a brutal 0.25-mile ascent, gaining 500 feet in elevation, and catch your breath at a narrow saddle.

From this saddle, repeat this exercise, with another 0.25-mile ascent and 500-foot gain to reach the ridgecrest just south of New York Peak. Scramble southwest among the boulders, keeping your eye out for a stand of white fir that grows in the company of pinyon pine.

If time, energy, and your abilities permit, continue along the rugged ridge to the summit. Otherwise, enjoy the marvelous view from the ridge. Broad Ivanpah Valley lies straight down to the north, and you'll be able to identify several prominent preserve features including Cima Dome to the west and Clark Mountain to the northwest. On very clear days, look for the high peaks of the San Bernardino and San Gabriel Mountains on the eastern border of the Los Angeles metropolitan area. The Virgin Mountains of southwestern Utah are located more than a 100 miles to the northeast.

With a careful eye for loose rock, retrace your route back to the trailhead.

18

Cima Dome

Eerie moonscape of the Cinder Cones area.

The triangle bounded by Kelbaker Road on the west, and Cima/Kelso Cima Road, which slants southwest to northwest, is a unique section of Mojave. Distinctive volcanic geology, cultural artifacts and botanical characteristics combine to make this area of particular interest to desert visitors.

During the late 1960s, this area was slated for inclusion in the state park system, but high construction costs for improvements —roads, campgrounds, facilities—led decision-makers to drop the site from consideration. Those who appreciate the wide-open spaces and wild quality of this area are no doubt grateful that it wasn't "improved."

Access to the heart of this area is on dirt

roads; although some high-clearance passenger vehicles might get you there, sport utility vehicles and pickup trucks are safer and more appropriate. Aiken Mine Road, the main road through the area, is usually well-graded, but it can be soft in spots. On your tour of the Cima Dome area, be sure to visit the tiny Cima General Store and Post Office.

CIMA DOME

Located just west of Cima Road, 25 miles due east of Baker, is the unique geologic formation known as Cima Dome. The almost-perfectly symmetrical dome is a geologic rarity, the most symmetrical natural dome feature in the United States. (If you have any doubt, take a look at the area's USGS topographical map and study the near-concentric contour lines.) This mass of once-molten monzonite, a granite-like rock, was uplifted by volcanic action;

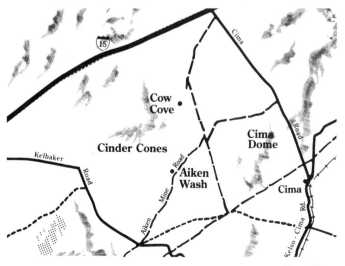

Cime Dome 223

over thousands of years it has been extensively eroded. The formation now covers some 75 square miles and rises nearly 1,500 feet above the 4,000-foot desert floor.

The rock outcroppings found here, particularly in the area of Teutonia Peak, are composed of the same type of rock that forms the distinctive, handsome rock outcroppings at Joshua Tree National Park to the south. Naturally, they are attractive to rock scramblers and rock-climbers. The remains of an old silver mine can still be seen at Teutonia Peak.

Mojave visitors are frequently confused about Cima Dome. Cima Dome is a place you drive on, not to. It's not a geologic formation you can view up-close; since the Dome slopes so gently, it's best viewed from a distance. The northernmost point at Mid Hills campground offers the best vantage point of Cima Dome, although it can also be viewed from Interstate 15, near Baker.

The Cima Dome area hosts the world's largest Joshua tree forest.

JOSHUA TREE FOREST

Atop Cima Dome is the site of the world's largest and densest Joshua tree forest. The most oft-repeated observation about the Joshua tree was made by 19th-century explorer John C. Frémont who called it "the most repulsive tree in the vegetable kingdom." Admittedly, the charms of a Joshua tree forest are unlike those of a stand of redwoods, but true desert rats consider the spiky tree a handsome feature of this dry land.

Yucca brevifolia, the Joshua tree, is actually a member of the lily family. Nothing about the plant gives a clue to its botanical bloodlines. Not its stiff stalks, shaggy trunk or towering height of 20 to 30 feet. This distinctive symbol of the Mojave Desert thrives at an elevation of about 4,000 feet. Although the trees are the most visible sign of life here, they shelter a thriving underbrush community of cholla and associated plants and animals.

Once proposed as a state park, Mojave's Joshua tree forest has long been a favorite attraction.

Mojave's Joshua trees belong to a slightly different subspecies than Joshuas that dwell in the southern and western Mojave Desert. The *Yucca brevifolia brevifolia* found in Joshua Tree National Park and the Yucca Valley are the largest trees, and have relatively long leaves. The *Yucca brevifolia jaegeriana* that thrives in Mojave National Preserve tends to be smaller and denser with smaller leaves.

The number of natural springs in the area attracts a variety of birds, including hawks, quail, and the loggerhead shrike. Cima Dome offers breeding habitat for the Bendire's Thrasher, and it's one of only two places in the California Desert where the Gilded Common Flicker lives (Clark Mountain, fifteen miles north is the other). Other animals include an assortment of reptiles and small mammals.

TEUTONIA PEAK TRAIL

You can experience both the famed Joshua Tree Forest and Cima Dome from

Teutonia Peak Trail (4 miles round trip with 600-foot elevation gain), one of the few signed and maintained footpaths in the preserve. The path is maintained by the San Gorgonio Chapter of the Sierra Club.

The trailhead for Teutonia Peak Trail is located just off Cima Road, a scenic preserve road that stretches 17 miles from the Cima Road exit on Interstate 15 south to Cima. The signed trailhead is on the west side of the road about 11 miles from I-15.

The mellow, two-mile Teutonia Peak Trail meanders across a sandy expanse through the Joshua tree forest. A mile out, you'll pass the remains of a mining operation and begin a moderate 0.25-mile ascent to the top of a ridge.

The trail follows the ridgecrest past stunted Joshuas, then junipers. A short scramble over some large boulders leads to the top of Teutonia Peak (elevation 5,755 feet). Enjoy the fine views of the preserve before retracing your steps back to the trailhead.

CINDER CONES

This 25,600-acre area has been designated a National Natural Landmark. Consisting of 32 volcanic formations, the cones are thought to date back 10 million years. These remnants of once-active vulcanism create an interesting, almost eerie red-black moonscape.

Legend has it that the Apollo astronauts trained on this moon-like surface in preparation for their historic 1969 lunar landing.

But officials deny that such maneuvers ever occurred. As you look out on this landscape, however, you can easily imagine the space-suited explorers bounding around on this moon-like surface, with the Cinder Cones in the background.

Neil Armstrong may not have taken even one small step for man on this volcanic field, but it does attract geologists from all over the world. The composition of the rock is said to be denser than anywhere on earth; it provides scientists with important information about geologic processes below the earth's surface.

The Aiken Mine has mined one of the cinder cones since the 1960s; the lightweight reddish material has literally been hauled away by the ton—it eventually ends up lining gardens and walkways of suburban homes and offices. Although some visitors consider the mine site a blight on the land, others are fascinated by the opportunity to peer into a cinder cone.

The petroglyphs of Cow Cove fascinate us. What is the significance of these figures?

COW COVE

Located about a five-mile hike into a wilderness area off Aiken Mine Road, Cow Cove is an outstanding petroglyph site that provides a glimpse into the culture of the past. Although little is known about the figures carved into these rocks, much is speculated. Today's visitors may imagine and attribute all sorts of meanings to the drawings that may be thousands of years old.

As you hike near the rocks, you'll view abstract figures and others that appear to have more literal meanings. Remember that these cultural artifacts, along with all other cultural resources in the Mojave, are protected by federal law. The Archeological Resources Protection Act of 1979 states that no person may "excavate, remove, damage, alter or deface any archeological resource." Fines for ignoring the law range up to $20,000 for a first offense, up to five years in jail for repeat offenders. Enjoy the site, but leave it undisturbed. Remember: The past belongs to the future, but only the present can preserve it.

AIKEN WASH

Located just off Aiken Mine Road, south of the Cinder Cones, is Aiken Wash, a favorite desert destination among those who enjoy getting off the beaten path. Also called Willow Wash for the large collection of large willow trees that thrives here, this wash runs through one of the most scenic areas of the preserve. The willows, Joshua trees and Mojave yucca, combined with the views of the nearby Cinder Cones and the solid black wall of basalt rock cut by the wash, make it a particularly memorable location. The willow-lined dry streambed is a lovely place to hike, especially in the springtime, when fragrant desert lavender is in full bloom.

The availability of surface water, the large assortment of edible cactus, and the abundance of trees at this site made it attractive to prehistoric people. There is evidence of human habitation in many cave-like areas near the wash, and many petroglyphs can be seen here. Like those at Cow Cove, five miles away, the cultural artifacts are protected by law.

Outside the entrance to the lava tube.

LAVA TUBE

For a memorable experience, explore the lava tube located in the cinder cone area on Aikens Mine Road some five miles north of its junction with Kelbaker Road.

During a long-ago volcanic eruption when swift-moving lava flowed over the land, the lava tube was formed when the inner flow cooled more quickly than the outer flow. Today, the resulting cave-like formation appears to be a great hole in the earth. A ladder in the tube facilitates climbing down into it; use caution as you maneuver into the tube. Making your way through the underground tube requires some bending and stretching; at one point explorers must flatten on the ground and

Ropy strands of pahoehoe lava remain from long ago volcanic eruptions.

Inside the lava tube, bathed in the strong light.

squeeze through a small opening to enter the great cave.

Bring a flashlight to explore the cave's nooks and crannies. The cool, dark underground area is a welcome retreat from the often-scorching outdoor temperatures and unrelenting sunlight; you're likely to spot bats or owls that inhabit the cave. Enjoy the unique setting, especially the beams of light that flood sections of the cave.

19

Clark Mountain

At 7,929 feet, Clark Mountain is the tallest peak in Mojave National Preserve. Because the peak is geographically isolated from the main part of the Clark Mountain Range situated to the northeast, it's a distinct and easy to recognize landmark when viewed from miles away.

Clark Mountain is also isolated from the main part of the preserve—the only section located north of I-15. The rugged mountain is one of the few places in Mojave to be crowned with a stand of white fir trees.

This handsome environment has been inhabited for thousands of years. Chemehuevi, Piute and Mohaves lived here. Archeologists have discovered a number of artifacts, including petroglyphs and rock

Mojave's tallest peak: 7,929-foot high Clark Mountain.

In less than 15 years, Clark Mountain's Lizzie Bullock Mine produced several million dollars worth of silver. The mine was played out by 1885.

shelters in the Clark Mountains. They have also found large ash-filled pits where native people once roasted agave for food. Experts speculate that native people may have considered the mountain spiritually significant.

Clark Mountain has been mined for more than a century; it produced more than four million 19th-century dollars worth of silver, along with significant amounts of gold, copper and several other rare, precious and semi-precious materials.

The town of Ivanpah was established on the slopes of Clark Mountain soon after three lucky propectors discovered a rich vein of silver in the mountain. A short-lived boomtown, the eastern Mojave's first, was founded in 1869; in 1875 its population was 500, mostly miners. By the end of the century, the town was abandoned. Only a few ruins of the fifteen buildings that once stood here still can be seen today.

Clark Mountain is the subject of one of the more colorful and enticing Mojave mining tales—the Lost River of Gold. A 1920s miner, Earl Dorr, tried to convince investors to finance his discovery in Crystal

Clark's pinyon pine shaded picnic area, a peaceful retreat.

Cave—a 3,000-foot-deep river through the mountain, its sands filled with gold.

Dorr managed to gain the backing of several wealthy Los Angeles speculators. He struck a rich vein, all right, but it was zinc, not gold. The Lost River has never been found, and today the mine is privately owned. The notion, however, of a Lost River of Gold continues to fascinate us.

These days most of the area's mining is concentrated near Mountain Pass located at the southern base of Clark Mountain. Long-established rare-earth mines operated by the Molybdenum Corporation of America (also known as Molycorp) produce elements useful in the high-tech manufacturing of such products as color TV tubes.

As for the slopes of the mountain itself, prospecting for turquoise and copper took place in the 1990s. Today the bulk of Clark Mountain is official preserve wilderness.

Clark Mountain has much to offer today's visitor in the way of scenic value and a diverse environment, but presents access difficulties. Roads to the mountain are dirt; road conditions can be quite variable and it should not be attempted in any vehicle except one suited to traveling on questionable roads.

One access to Clark Mountain is off I-15 at Mountain Pass. There you'll view the Molycorp Mine, a long-established rare-earth mine. The dirt road just past the one-room elementary school is the main access to Clark Mountain. It leads past Joshuas and rises into a landscape of junipers and pinyon pine.

Clark Mountain is combed with many rough dirt roads - take along a good map.

At the end of the road (there are many roads here so it is sometimes difficult to follow the main road), you'll find a handsome picnic area, complete with barbeque pits, picnic tables and a volleyball court, all nestled in a pinyon pine forest. The facilities were established here by Molycorp many years ago. The company formerly held its annual family picnic at the Clark Mountain site.

Today, the spot is a lovely place to picnic, or to use as a jumping-off spot for further exploration. Bighorn sheep thrive here, as do raptors and several snakes and lizards.

Another way to reach Clark Mountain is by way of the powerline road that extends east-west back of the mountain along the far northern boundary of the preserve. You can reach this road by exiting Interstate 15 on paved Excelsor Mine Road and traveling 7.7 miles to the graded powerline road. Turn right and travel 6 miles to a rougher road that follows a wash south to the mountain.

This road will intersect with another dirt road that travels east-west along the backside of Clark Mountain. This is an excellent area to explore. Some short dead-end roads lead up to beautiful wooded areas where small campsites are located. Please observe the wilderness boundary signs where only foot or horse travel is allowed. The old abandoned rocky roads that go into the wilderness are excellent for hiking up to higher spots on the mountain. Watch for desert bighorn sheep in the high country throughout this area. The best direction to travel on the east-west road is to the east, which takes you past the old Coliseum Mine and back to Mountain Pass at I-15.

You can also join the powerline road from Primm (formerly Stateline), Nevada. Exit I-15, head over to the west side of the highway. Drive 0.5 mile west away from the casinos and Ivanpah Dry Lake, which spreads south and east. At a junction, bear north 0.9 mile to intersect the powerline road. The good gravel road leads some 10 miles as it ascends 4,906-foot Keany Pass. On clear days, enjoy far reaching views over Nevada. Continue west on the powerline road and past a right-forking road that leads to Mesquite Pass and down the Mesquite Mountains to Mesquite Dry Lake. About 0.8 mile past Mesquite Pass Road, you'll junction a rough road leading south toward Clark Mountain.

Ascend amidst Joshua trees, pinyon pine, juniper and scores of cacti. About 3.4 miles from the powerline road, bear left at a junction and drive 2 miles to Coliseum Gorge, where you'll get a great close-up view of Clark Mountain's upper slopes to the south.

Hikers can utilize a number of rough dirt roads ascending the mountain. Stay on preserve lands and heed the various private property/no trespassing signs.

Experienced four-wheel drive enthusiasts descend east from Clark Mountain back to Interstate 15; it's a challenging route. We recommend you return the way you came by way of the powerline road.

Ranger James Woolsey atop Clark Mountain

Resources

Mojave National Preserve Headquarters
222 E. Main St., Suite 202
Barstow, CA 92311
(760) 255-8801
Mojave Desert
Needles Information Center
707 W. Broadway
Needles, CA 92363
(760) 326-6322
Mojave Desert
Baker Information Center
72157 Baker Blvd.
(P.O. Box 241)
Baker, CA 92309
(760) 733-4040
Hole-in-the-Wall Ranger Station
(760) 928-2572

Barstow
(888) 4-BARSTOW (422-
7786)

California Welcome Center
2796 Tanger Way, Suite 100
Barstow, CA 92311
(760) 253-4813

**Calico Early Man
Archeological Site**
P.O. 535
Yermo, CA 92398

**California Desert Studies
Center Consortium**
c/o California State Univeristy,
Fullerton
P.O. Box 6850
Fullerton, CA 92834
(714) 278-2428

Friends of the Mojave Road
Goffs Schoolhouse
37198 Lanfair Road G-15
Essex, CA 92332
(760) 734-4482

**Granite Mountains Natural
Reserve**
University of California,
Riverside
P.O. Box 101
Kelso, CA 92351

**Mojave River Valley
Museum**
270 East Virginia Way
Barstow, CA 92311
(760) 256-5452

Nipton Station
Route #1, Box 357
Nipton, CA 92364
(760) 856-2335

**Providence Mountains State
Recreation Area**
Post Office Box 1
Essex, Ca 92332
(760) 928-2586

**U.S. Bureau of Land
Management
Afton Canyon**
(760) 252-6060

California Desert District
6221 Box Spring Blvd.
Riverside, CA 92507
(909) 697-5200

Needles Resource Area
101 W. Spike's Road
Needles, CA 92363
(760) 326-3896

Index